M000214932

THE 1993 WORLD TRADE CENTER BOMBING
Foresight and Warning

PETER CARAM

JANUS PUBLISHING COMPANY
London, England

First published in Great Britain 2001 by
Janus Publishing Company Ltd,
76 Great Titchfield Street,
London W1P 7AF

www.januspublishing.co.uk

Copyright © 2001 by Peter Caram
The author has asserted his moral rights

British Library Cataloguing-in-Publication Data
A catalogue record for this book
is available from the British Library

ISBN 1 85756 586 X

Typeset in 11pt Baskerville
By Chris Cowlin

Cover design Michael Dickinson

Printed and bound in Great Britain

To
Madeline, Chris and Courtney
For your love, inspiration and understanding

CONTENTS

INTRODUCTION

This book was nine years in the making. I didn't start writing it until I retired from the Port Authority Police Department in February of 1998. I knew I had to tell the story only a few select individuals were privy to. There is little doubt in anyone's mind that the devastating blast of February 26, 1993, at the Port Authority-owned World Trade Center in the heart of the financial district of New York City was a blow to the security and serenity of the American public. This book will reveal how, for many years prior to the bombing of the World Trade Center, the Port Authority of New York and New Jersey ignored and miscalculated warnings from their own experts and consultants regarding the vulnerability of some of the world's tallest buildings. The general public and the families of those individuals who died and were injured have never had the closure they deserve to their life-altering nightmare.

I have endeavored to assimilate into my writings an unprejudiced approach and an understanding of various disciplines including academic, religious and security and tied these into vulnerability assessments. The consideration of intelligence reports and of the internal political apparatus of the Port Authority exposes a schism in the decision-making by the leadership and management of the agency.

There has been a mass of written information regarding the 'causes of the bombing.' We attempt to develop some coherent model which helps explain the events of the past. Gary Sick, in his book *October Surprise*, states it best: 'The process of remembrance and reconstruction is notoriously difficult and inherently faulty, but even a partly true, or at least convincing, version of the past is usually preferred to no explanation at all.

Although we can never know the complex series of human acts, we can strive for enough truth to reasonably satisfy both our curiosity and our hunger to understand the peculiar path history has taken.' (*October Surpise*, Gary Sick, Random House April 1991, introduction.)

The Port Authority is a bi-state agency. It was formed by an Act of Congress in 1921, consented to in a joint resolution. The Port Authority was originally formed and empowered to act as the region's planner for economic gain and prosperity. Its legal boundaries fall within a twenty-five mile radius of the Statue of Liberty. Thus the term 'port district.' The original plan was for The Port Authority to 'operate without burden to the taxpayer.' The mandate was for the agency 'to deal with the continuous planning and development of terminal and transportation facilities, and to improve and protect the commerce of the Port District.' The facilities which comprise the Port District are the Holland and Lincoln Tunnels, the George Washington, Goethals, Bayonne bridges. The Port Authority also operates John F. Kennedy, LaGuardia, Newark, and Teteboro Airports. Included under the Port Authority's umbrella are also the Wall Street Heliport and the 30th Street Heliport. The PATH rail system between New Jersey and the Port Authority Bus Terminal along with the Port of Newark, and Port of Elizabeth are also Port Authority operated.

The World Trade Center opened in 1973. The complex occupied a sixteen acre plot of land in downtown Manhattan. The twin towers construction cost about US$750 million. The twin skyscrapers consisted of 13 million square feet. The towers were reported to be 1,350 feet tall and had some where in the vicinity of 30,000 windows. There were 104 elevators and about an acre of space per floor. The center housed approximately 100,000 working people with many thousands more visiting and traveling to various locations in downtown Manhattan. The subgrade level included approximately 2,000 parking spaces, some for tenants and others for public use. The B-1 level housed the emergency control center occupied by the Port Authority Police Unit and Fire Control Board and communications complex.

The blast in 1993 occurred on the B-2 level, which was used mostly for parking. This blast created a crater approximately 11,500 square feet in size. The explosion occurred directly below the police and fire communications control center, rendering the public safety systems useless.

The Port Authority must admit that there were plenty of alarms sounded with respect to the vulnerability to car bombs of public parking at the World Trade Center. The Authority in 1992 allegedly spent US$10,000 on a study on how to increase revenue from public parking instead of limiting access. According to William Hataway of the National Transportation Center, which is a private consulting firm in Cambridge, Massachusetts, 'most security incidents are preventable, if you can get any one to pay attention to terrorism. It is a matter of trading money off against what you perceive as a threat.'

Acknowledgements

I wish to acknowledge the many law enforcement and intelligence officials who encouraged me to document my experiences. I respect their wish to remain anonymous, and express my gratitude to them for their respect and courage in providing valuable information and insight.

I also acknowledge: the current and past Port Authority employees who are the strength and pillars of the Port Authority, and my colleagues of the Port Authority Police Department who daily strive to provide a safe environment to the millions of people entering and traveling through our great country. To them I say: although your action is rarely proclaimed, your performance is unequaled. Also, the Plaintiffs' Steering Committee and especially their Liaison Counsel who have tirelessly persevered in the courts to obtain justice for the injured and damaged.

If circumstances lead me, I will find
Where truth is hid, though it were hid indeed
Within the center.

Shakespeare, Hamlet

CHAPTER 1
The Reason for Panic

As I lay on the couch watching the wind-blown snow whip against my family room window, the crackling of my fireplace brought the only relief to an otherwise miserable day. It was that time of year – I had bronchitis again, a twice yearly malady, compliments of working at Kennedy and Newark airports. The medication was taking its toll. I was drowsy and lethargic, congested and bored. My beeper is usually off, but this day I decided to leave it on. As I drifted into the abyss of a welcome deep sleep, bingo, the beeper sounded. The number was a recall from the Joint Terrorist Task Force in New York City. Only this time it was accentuated with '991' followed with a '1' to indicate an actual happening. The voice on the other end was familiar to me, and the first question was, 'Can you go secure?' 'No,' I replied, 'I am home sick.' 'OK', was the response. A few seconds later the message was clear. 'What the hell are you talking about?' I asked. 'Listen Abdul (my affectionate name to the FBI), they just blew up the World Trade Center. When can you get your butt in here?'

My mind raced uncontrollably. My heart was in my mouth. I was no longer bored. 'I will be in on Monday, that's the earliest,' I replied sheepishly. I barely had time to put the television on when the telephone rang again. 'Pete, you're needed right away,' was the message from the trembling voice on the other end. 'I am too sick to leave the house, who wants me?' The deputy director of the Port Authority Police wanted access to my safe at work in order to remove some documents. 'Advise him he cannot access the safe because it contains national security information and equipment and he is not cleared. Any attempt

1

to breach and enter will result in his arrest for unauthorized access and disclosure of classified information.' I suspected he was looking for something that in the future would add to the Port Authority's misinformation campaign.

I sat on my couch, trying to gain some composure while listening to the news reports, replete with speculation and guessing. This seemed to be typical 'panic journalism' by the New York media. The telephone rang again and this time it was Detective Matt Besheer who worked for me in the Terrorist Intelligence Unit. 'Pete you must have heard by now what is going on. The deputy director and chief are in the office and want all of the World Trade Center security studies and accompanying documents.' 'What is their reasoning?' I asked. 'They want to make sure there isn't unauthorized disclosure. To this I responded, 'What bullshit – however, give them what they want, but they cannot go into the safe. Call me later Matt.' The telephone went flying across the room.

Here I am, the supervisor of the Terrorist Intelligence Unit of the Port Authority Police Department, a quasi-governmental agency and owner of the World Trade Center in New York City. I have been the supervisor for ten years, hold a top secret security clearance, am known to every intelligence gathering group in the US and overseas, and these two individuals can't trust me with the security survey? No, that's not it. The reason for the request is that the information in the report is critical and they must control the report, an act consistent with damage control. Why?

The Sunday after the bombing of the Trade Center found me on my way to the office at Journal Square to meet with the deputy director of public safety and some Port Authority officials. The purpose of the meeting was to deliver to the deputy director all of the security studies and supporting documents relating to the World Trade Center. My anger was tempered by the medication I was taking for my bronchitis. The news reports from my car radio were constant, with new theories and conspiracies being reported every five minutes by the media. I entered my office to be greeted by Detectives Besheer and Anderson of my unit, the deputy director of public safety, and a representative from the Port Authority Law Department. We exchanged greetings after which I was informed that they wanted all of the security studies and reports for the World Trade Center.

In order for one to appreciate this situation, a brief overview of the workings of the Public Safety Department of the Port Authority is in order. The Public Safety Department is the Police Department of the Port Authority. We are 1,500 highly trained men and women who have law enforcement jurisdiction in both the States of New York and New Jersey. Our command structure consists of both uniform officers and detectives with the highest-ranking uniform officer being the chief. The director of public safety and deputy director are appointed by the executive director of the Port Authority. These two positions are usually political appointments. The Port Authority's mindset could be summed up as: 'We answer to no one.' Therefore, the presence and direct request for the security studies by these individuals was completely in character. Being the cooperative individual that I am, I turned over all the available documents to the deputy director of public safety. However, I did ask one question, 'What about the copies at the World Trade Center?' They responded, 'What? What copies?' Laughing to myself, I went on to explain to the number two guy in the Department of Public Safety that copies were given to the executive director and deputy executive director of the Port Authority for their review and comments. The legal representative advised me that they would have to 'check on that.' After the deputy director and legal representative left, I sat down with my two trusted detectives and analyzed the real reason behind the seizure of the reports. The Port Authority was not concerned with identification of the person who detonated the bomb, our opinion, the number of dead and injured, or the progress of the investigation. They were concerned only with the existence and circulation of the reports. The answer was becoming clearer by the second: damage control, denial, misinformation and, ultimately, placing the blame on someone else.

The actions of the deputy director and Law Department were consistent with any large corporation trying to mitigate future lawsuits. However, the Port Authority is a public agency that answers to the people. 'How naive am I?' I thought to myself. 'Good reason to panic! The information in those security studies is damaging to the Port Authority. No question about it! What is so critically important about security studies? Were the proposed recommendations implemented? Who rejected the recommendations? Why were they rejected? Could the World Trade Center bombing have been prevented?'

The purpose of any intelligence unit is to obtain information so police commanders can make decisions to enhance public safety. The Terrorist Intelligence Unit of the Port Authority Police Department was unique. Its function was to gather information and make recommendations to prevent potential terrorist activity against all of the Port Authority facilities, which for the most part were transportation facilities. Historically, transportation facilities have been the focus of international terrorists more than any other non-military target.

That is why, on January 4, 1984, I had written a memo to the assistant superintendent of police at the Port Authority, indicating that a terrorist threat had been uncovered by the Federal Bureau of Investigation. Information had been developed by the Bureau that two individuals allegedly had targeted the World Trade Center for a bombing in the near future. The two subjects of the investigation were loyalists to the Ayatollah Khomeini. The source of the information was a third party informant whose information had never been tested. I

4

made the necessary notifications to the commanding officer at the World Trade Center and monitored developments of the threat, which never materialized. I was directed by the Assistant Superintendent of Police to develop a report regarding 'The Vulnerability of the World Trade Center to Terrorist Attack'.

On January 17, 1984, I completed my preliminary review of the World Trade Center in a four page synopsis entitled 'Terrorist Threat and Targeting Assessment: World Trade Center'. I gave a copy to the commanding officer at the World Trade Center and the assistant superintendent of police. The report addressed several areas of concern including the reasoning behind the targeting of the World Trade Center for terrorist attack. I focused on the vulnerability of the subgrade and parking levels. My physical inspection of the World Trade Center was not difficult since I had been a patrol sergeant and operations sergeant at the complex for many years prior.

Specifically, the targeted areas of review were the subgrade, the truck dock, and the perimeter of the complex. All three areas were vulnerable to any form of terrorist attack. The most vulnerable was the subgrade area. I cited the 1983 truck bombing of the US Marine barracks in Beirut, Lebanon, and the method of attack – a truck loaded with 12,000 pounds of explosives. The truck dock is under the control of civilian security guards with no training in counter-terrorist operations, let alone discovery techniques or bomb and explosive recognition. These elements reduced the protective shield around the World Trade Center and allowed penetration to the subgrade, equivalent to a walk in the park for a half trained terrorist.

The subgrade area was a shopping mall for any terrorist with an explosive-laden vehicle. It was virtually unprotected except for a security guard augmenting one police officer. My report was clear. The subgrade was completely vulnerable and immediate attention should be paid to increasing security in the

5

area. I also recommended that all security functions be placed under the control of the police commanding officer at the World Trade Center. The system in place at the time was fragmented and very political – what could you expect?

In 1986 I received through the US Department of State Office of Diplomatic Security in New York a very credible threat to the PATH Train system that operated underground at the World Trade Center. As part of my liaison duties, I met weekly with special agent in charge Patrick O'Hanlon to discuss VIP movements and international incidents and intelligence. This was especially critical since most of the diplomats entering New York to attend the United Nations sessions utilized Port Authority facilities. Information had been developed overseas by 'intelligence sources' that a Middle Eastern group was looking at a possible bombing of the PATH rail system at the World Trade Center. I was directed by the superintendent of police to conduct a joint investigation with the State Department and the FBI Joint Terrorist Task Force. In order to determine the credibility of the informant, I developed a list of questions to determine the level of knowledge regarding the target. The answers would show if the informant indeed had sufficient knowledge, which he had garnered from the terrorist group. Intelligence agents interviewed the informant at an overseas location. Upon completion I reviewed the tape recording of the interview as did the superintendent and assistant superintendent of police, the commanding officer of the police command at PATH, the manager of PATH, and engineering personnel. Our conclusion was that the informant was better than 90 percent accurate with regard to targeting information, thus verifying the seriousness and credibility of the threat. What was really emerging was that without the informant's cooperation there existed a high probability of a successful terrorist attack upon the crowded rail system.

A high ranking police commander once told me during a

meeting, 'If you make a recommendation and we do not address it or implement it and something goes wrong, it's our ass since you are the terrorist expert making the recommendation.'

Over the next several years, I filtered reports regarding terrorism, especially in the Middle East, to the command staff of the Port Authority Police Department. With each warning and recommendation, my fears and doubts increased. Such remarks as 'Can you prove this information is reliable?' or 'This happened overseas, it can't happen here', indicated the basis for policy formulation by those individuals responsible for public safety.

In connection with my continuing efforts to follow the threat of terrorism, during the middle of March 1992, I wrote a position paper outlining Militant Islam. The report covered the increased activity levels by Militant Islamists in Saudi Arabia, Afghanistan, Algeria and Lebanon. I specifically documented groups such as the Hezballah, Islamic Jihad, and the Muslim Brotherhood. I hoped that the report would assist commanders to develop an understanding of the methodology of terrorism employed by these groups and to manage potential problems before they occured. To my dismay, I had discovered that police commanders in the US did not even know the difference between the Shia and Sunni Muslims, and they did not have enough information regarding the ethos of these groups to make informed decisions.

This prevailing attitude was understandable since there was very little interest, I found, in Middle Eastern terrorism on the local scale except for media reporting. However, the federal agencies had explored a different approach. They had at least questioned the efficiency of establishing a unit specifically tasked to track and follow events relative to, and associated with, Middle Eastern terrorism, in the context of protecting the traveling public.

Well, the Port Authority took an exceptually confident approach. A memo originating in headquarters claimed that terrorism was at an all time low and that the Terrorist Unit should be reassigned. This, despite the fact that only a day before a memo had been prepared which indicated there was a bombing in New York City in a building near the United Nations which housed a Middle Eastern embassy office. A Port Authority commander requested a member from Port Authority Management and Engineering to prepare a full study on the Terrorist Unit, with the results repeating those of an original memo written earlier.

The ineptness of the Port Authority leadership and the fragmented security system was highlighted by events on a Friday in January 1993. On that day I was at Sing Sing Prison in New York State. My purpose there was to conduct an eight hour training class for members of the New York State Department of Corrections. The subject was 'Understanding Islam And Methods of Management.' There were some 200 Corrections Officers from various prisons present, and the lecture and training were well received. While I was driving home, I was beeped by the police commander at the World Trade Center. He had received a telephone warning from the Joint Terrorist Task Force in New York regarding the potential bombing of a high rise in New York City. He requested that I verify the information and develop further leads, if there were any. I called the Joint Terrorist Task Force and, since I could not go secure, I received the unclassified version. Somewhere in the Middle East, two telephone calls had been received indicating there would be a bombing of a high rise in New York within the next thirty days. When I spoke with the commander of the World Trade Center, he voiced concerns as to the nature and validity of the threat. I told him that I felt the threat was within the guidelines for an immediate increase in perimeter and subgrade patrols until the threat period expired and more information could be garnered. The ultimate reduction of increased police patrols was a result of overtime costs and management's reluctances to incur the extra financial burden, despite the viable threat. During the next few weeks, information regarding the threat was not forthcoming and, like the man said, 'if you recommend and we don't follow, it's our butts.'

CHAPTER 2
Indifference or Ignorance

On February 27, 1993, the day after the blast at the World Trade Center, an article by Martin Gottlieb appeared in the *New York Times*. This article was most interesting because it contained quotes from Port Authority executives regarding the failure of the evacuation plan and other essential emergency services. The former director of the Port Authority was quoted in the article as stating, 'the Port Authority had commissioned studies on terrorist attacks against the World Trade Center and concluded the Trade Center could withstand a car bombing in the underground garage.' He further stated, 'They said you could sustain a car bomb', and 'what they didn't tell us was you couldn't sustain it if it was perfectly placed.' This statement exemplifies the attitude and direction the Port Authority planned to follow as a method of deflecting accountability and responsibility, at least contributory responsibility, for the tragic bombing. There must be something written in those reports which would hint at moving the police desk and emergency control center from the B-1 level to the 310 level, also known as street level. Probably just another recommendation. Who would want the emergency control center away from the basement level where it could be exposed to a potential truck or car bomb?

Good Intentions – the Establishment of the Office of Special Planning

Logic and necessity were the reasons behind the development of the Office of Special Planning (OSP). World terrorism was abundant, and the United States was becoming more vulnerable by the day. With international terrorism targeting public transportation facilities two-thirds of the time, the Port Authority was to be commended for realizing the potential for terrorist attacks against its facilities. Prior to the development of the OSP, I had been directed by the director of public safety, John Giovanni, to assist police commanders in the development of their hostage and terrorist emergency response plans. I was further directed to develop, with these commanders, a critical vulnerability study of their commands. This concept was put into effect on October 20, 1982. Only one problem. I had no secretarial or manpower assigned to assist me in this task. I felt as if I was the 'symbolic target' in this venture.

Trying to get the commanding officers to submit their vulnerability studies was an adventure. Understandably, they did not have the expertise nor the manpower to identify properly all their targets and divide them into 'critical versus non-critical.' Trying to balance their needs with the deadlines of the director of public safety I found the job was not getting done with the urgency that was required. I voiced my concerns several times. I continued to assist the commanding officers while gathering terrorist intelligence information from numerous sources. My database grew. My network and unclassified review of terrorist activity worldwide on a real time schedule expanded and intensified. Our vulnerability study program was, however, lacking. At this point, the executive director of the Port Authority, Peter Goldmark, formally established the Office for Special Planning.

This special unit was a necessity born out of fear of the potential catastrophic effects of a terrorist attack and the knowledge that the Port Authority and its facilities were open and subject to attack at any time. What was really scary was that there was little available within the Police Unit to offset such an attack. This was not the fault of the Police Unit but rather the policy formulated by those in charge of the Port Authority. The Port Authority's position was clear – it can't happen here and if it does, let the New York City Police Department or some other unit come in and clean it up. Thus, the Port Authority's planning and response to a terrorist attack was extremely limited. Respond and hold the situation. Take no action, understandably, since the training and equipment to manage such an incident was limited. Our police officers were under-staffed and under gunned in these situations. We were fortunate that there was no frontal assault comparable to the one at the Vienna Airport. It would have been a bloodbath.

The Office of Special Planning had developed an expertise unmatched in the United States. The manager, Edward O'Sullivan, a decorated US Marine and career Port Authority employee, was selected to head the unit. He was assisted by Captain Frank Fox, a career police official with extensive service and experience. Both of these gentlemen were professionalism personified. Police officers and Port Authority civilians working together, filled the roster. I did not work directly with the unit as a result of labor issues within the Port Authority. We claimed the unit should have been staffed by sergeants since I had been doing the work for years prior to the establishment of the Office for Special Planning. This conflict went on for years and I continued to do my terrorist intelligence work outside of the Office for Special Planning. This type of fragmented approach to handling potential terrorist problems was not only ineffective, but alienated many of the police and civilian managers who received information from two sources.

Ultimately, the Port Authority conceded before an arbitrator and the Sergeant's Union won the unit work issue; O'Sullivan and Captain Fox were reassigned. The other members were promoted, or left the Port Authority for other careers. I inherited a staff of two detectives, two civilians and Grace, our secretary. We continued with the work which had been started, and finished the rest of the vulnerability studies. Once completed, we started to audit the facilities for compliance and implementation of recommendations. By this time, I had lost the two civilians and Grace. I was left with my two detectives and an answering machine to conduct the work of seven people. The Port Authority refused to allocate sufficient manpower to ensure the success of the program. It had become a smoke and screen endeavor. Disgusted with the lack of cooperation from facility managers and lack of support from my own commanders, I fired off a stinging memo to the Director of Public Safety through my Captain, James O'Neill. The memo was dated December 11, 1991. I never received the courtesy of a reply.

I continued to seek assistance for my unit, but my requests fell on deaf ears. Without the additional support needed to complete the audits, my unit found itself strictly in the terrorist intelligence business. We had been given additional duties in the area of organized crime activity at the World Trade Center and spent over a year investigating the murder of Louie Dubono, a John Gotti employee. This case was conducted in conjunction with the New York State Organized Crime Task Force. With our attention focused in this area, the counter terrorist effort faded away except for the intelligence gathering.[1]

On March 16, 1992, I wrote a memo called 'Militant Islam – An Overview' and addressed it to Captain James O'Neill. The report was an overview of terrorist activities in the Middle East caused by the two most visible and emerging terrorist groups, the Hezballah (Party of God) and the Muslim Brotherhood. Saudi Arabia, Algeria and Lebanon were highlighted as being the recipients of the increased activity of these groups. I found out later that the report was sent to file and never circulated to the police commands for their information.

The Office for Special Planning, the Port Authority's in-house Terrorist Task Force had, for some six years prior to the bombing, made many recommendations regarding the vulnerability of the Trade Center, and the efforts and actions that should be taken to shore up the weaknesses. The World Trade Center Director Charles Makish, at a news conference on Sunday, February 28, 1993, said, 'It, [meaning the report] found basically, that the subterranean garage levels are capable of sustaining a car bomb.' Unidentified Port Authority officials went on to admit the existence of the report, but could not comment until they read a copy of it. It certainly seems remarkable that top executives of the Port Authority and the World Trade Center did not know what that report said about the security condition of the most symbolic target in the United States. Who was in charge? Where was the accountability?

They all received medals for putting the Trade Center back together. It seems that it was taken as correct that they had not prohibited public parking to prevent terrorists from placing a car bomb in the parking lot, or damaging the power supply, and that they had not moved the police station and command center, or installed battery backup lighting in the stairwells. I never understood why we had a task force and terrorist intelligence if the Port Authority ignored our recommendations and intelligence reports. Damage limitation, deflection of blame, ignorance of the facts maybe? Sounds a little harsh? I reason that the Port Authority, one of the most powerful and autonomous entities in the country, refuses to come clean about the bombing. The public and those families of the unfortunate victims have a right to know why they lost loved ones and why they were injured.

The Subpoena after the Bombing

Having been a law enforcement officer for twenty-five years, I felt no excitement at receiving a subpoena to testify in a case.

Most of my cases ended up being plea-bargained and never ended in trial. On March 17, 1993, a month after the bombing, I received a subpoena to testify before the New York State Senate Committee on Taxation and Government Operations. The accompanying letter was signed by Rachel Gordon, Chief Investigative Counsel to state senator and Chairman Roy M. Goodman. The Senator, a no-nonsense Republican, impanelled a committee to investigate the bombing. He reminded me of the Republican old guard of Brooklyn where I grew up, staunch, serious and articulate. I followed the established protocol and notified the appropriate people in the Port Authority, including the Law Department, of the subpoena. 'The subpoena required that I bring with me all relevant documents, reports, and memoranda.' I queried my ability to bring what I didn't have.

A few days before I was to testify, I was summoned to a meeting at 7 World Trade Center, the temporary headquarters of the Port Authority. When I entered the conference room, I noted it was a far cry from the corporate opulence of the real World Trade Center. The air in the room was icy; figures were withdrawn, nervous faces filled the room. Present in the room were Charles Knox, Director of Public Safety; Captain Tom Farrell; my captain, Inspector James O'Neill; Chief Jack Boland, my immediate supervisor; and a host of Port Authority lawyers and public relations mouthpieces. I knew they weren't there to promote me, and it certainly wasn't an intelligence briefing they wanted. Usually, when I attended these types of high level meetings, I had very little to say. Today was different. As usual, no one asked how I was feeling (elite management style is not compassionate). The committee was worried. It showed on their faces. I was going to testify, and the fear of what I was going to say had them unnerved.

I went on the offensive. 'Clearly gentlemen, your concern as to the facts is justified. However, my position is rather simple. I

15

will answer all questions truthfully and to the best of my knowledge.' Director Knox was leaving on vacation the next day, and really was not interested in what I was going to do or say. One of the attorneys wanted to know specifics about documents and testimony. I politely informed him that I had no documents in my possession, that the Law Department and Public Safety had confiscated them days before. His eyes became enlarged. He continued to ask about documents and reports, never accepting my answer. Although unsatisfied, his questioning focused on what exactly I was going to tell the committee. I said, 'The truth!' He started to raise his voice in frustration and I cut him off with an outburst of outspoken anger. Chief Boland told me to cool down and remember where I was and to whom I was speaking. The representative from Public Affairs, Mark Marchese, asked me to step outside for a moment. I had known Mark for many years and although I despised his occupation, I respected the man for his honesty with me. He said, 'Pete, I have known you a long time, this is a no-win situation for you.' To this I responded, 'What are you talking about Mark?' He replied, in a soft, monotone voice, 'The Law Department is looking for some reasonable answers, that is all.'

'Mark, how can I tell them what my answers will be if I haven't yet been asked any questions by the committee? Are all of them such fools or just paranoid?'

'They are under the gun,' he said. 'The Director and former Directors of the Port Authority are all going to testify, and your testimony cannot be in conflict with theirs.' I started to get the picture. 'Mark,' I said, with deliberation and sincerity, 'I do not fabricate, lie, or support misinformation.' His reply was, 'I did not ask these things of you; no one would.' My eyes pierced his body as I asked him, 'What is it that I have to do to placate the politburo inside?'

'Try and cooperate with suggestive forms of answers.'

'Mark, I have a reputation, and I am sworn to protect the public. I am not bound by the internal politics of the feeble minded.'

I went back into the room, and discovered that during this interval they had brought in some coffee and pastries, which I could not take since I am a diabetic. At this point I knew I could and would not back down, but on that occasion I would tell them what they wanted to hear. I entertained the committee with lapses in memory, and answers of no serious consequence. I believed that my career was over.

The next day I called Rachel Gordon, Chief Investigative Counsel, and asked for an appointment to see her about the subpoena. The following day we met for lunch downtown on Broadway. She was articulate, smart and understanding. I explained that I had no documents, that they had been removed, and that I would be testifying by memory only. She understood and only asked that I tell the truth. She had done her homework. 'I am familiar with your national security clearance level and the work you have done for years in the area of counter terrorism. You are a credit to yourself and the Port Authority Police Department. Your colleagues in law enforcement hold you in the highest regard', was her remarks to me as I devoured my tuna fish sandwich and diet soda. I left her at the restaurant and walked north on Broadway to 26 Federal Plaza, home of the Joint Terrorist Task Force.

That evening, as I sat in traffic on the New Jersey Turnpike, I started to analyze the repercussions of my potential testimony. My heart increased its steady rhythm, I experienced chills, I thought I was back in Vietnam. Was I experiencing an internal conflict between my desire to tell the truth and an unacceptable form of corrupt loyalty to the organization? Who wins if I alter the truth? My career? The Port Authority politicians? What about my oath to protect the public? People died, thousands were injured. What is to be gained by loss of memory? I am likely to end up under a rock just like the rest of them. The traffic finally broke, my breathing eased, I wanted to get home and hug my family.

CHAPTER 3
Understanding the Adversary

One of the most indelible misconceptions about Islam is that all its adherents, one billion strong of them, are Islamic terrorists. This concept was fostered by not only the Western media, but also by the hierarchy of Western intelligence services.

It is a great injustice to label all believers of Islam as 'terrorists'. In order to manage our adversaries, whether their motives are geopolitical, religious, transnational or revolutionary, one must strive to understand their mindset, their cultural, religious, historical, and customary beliefs. An understanding of these elements is necessary to produce an objective model leading to an impartial analysis.

I have endeavored through many years to understand the mindset of the Middle Eastern terrorist, what motivates his thinking, and what his ultimate goals are in the world arena. I have performed this analysis through the reading of the Holy Quran, other writings by Islamic leaders, philosophers, and Mullahs, and writings by Western academics and intelligence sources, to balance out the extremes.

The Significance of Islam
One of the first elements I offered in teaching law enforcement to elite military units was a basic understanding and interpretation of what I believe Islam signifies. This approach creates an unbiased foundation, and hopefully eradicates prejudices already ingrained by a biased media.

Islam is basically defined as the religion of peace. The word 'Islam' literally means peace or submission. It consists of a complete, unobstructed loyalty and submission to the teachings and will of Allah.

Islam has many attributes, knowing just a few of which enable the reader to remove preconceived notions and misunderstandings of the religion. Islam is described as the only complete way of life for the betterment of mankind. It provides the only total unifying force available to the human species. It is the only system for implementing purity, justice and excellence in moral, spiritual, economic, social and political affairs through a system of equality.

Islam is a pure religion. Its object is to provide believers and adherents with a perfect code allowing for a more noble and gentle means of conflict resolution and the maintenance of a balanced peace between brethren. The Quran is the Holy Scripture of Islam. The Muslims believe in the divine origins of other religions, their scriptures and apostles. In essence, Islam teaches tolerance of other religions, including the Christian–Judeo ethic.

There are seven articles of faith within the great teachings of Islam. The first article of faith is the undeniable belief in Allah, or God. The other six are: the book from Allah; the Angel; the messenger from Allah; the Hereafter; the ability to pre-measure good from evil and the resurrection after death.

We often hear of what are called the Pillars of Islam. These Pillars are also part of the foundation of belief in Islam. They are: the declaration of faith in Allah, who is great, and there is only one God, and He is Allah; Prayer, Fasting, Charity, and the once-in-a-person's-lifetime pilgrimage to the Holy Ka-ba, the house of Allah in the city of Mecca, in Saudi Arabia.

Another important element of Islam is faith and action. This doctrine basically states that faith is academic unless translated into action. In other words, deeds outperform verbal arguments. A Muslim should believe in his own accountability for his actions, in the present and hereafter. He must bear his own burden for his actions and no one can expiate another's sins. The equality of mankind and the brotherhood of Islam are vital elements in the makeup of Islam. Now this statement may seem confusing since we are conditioned to equate Islam with terrorism. I will explain the phenomenon in general terms.

Islam is the religion of the unity of Allah and the equality of mankind. It is widely held that lineage, riches, and family honors are accidental happenings in people's lives whereas virtue and service to humanity are matters of real merit. Most important is that the status of race, color and creed are of no consequence. Knowledge and the pursuit of knowledge are duties. Muslims believe that the acquisition of knowledge makes a man superior to angels. When it comes to defining labor and work, Islam is very specific. Any honest labor which allows a man to live by his means is highly respected. Laziness or idleness is sinful. Under Islam, charity and giving to the poor is obligatory.

The significance of the Holy Quran and the impact on the everyday life of the Muslim is necessary for a complete understanding of this culture. The Holy Quran is not a single, focused document by which a man must guide his everyday life. The Holy Quran, much to the surprise of the average Westerner, is a political and legal document, contributing to the everyday harmony of a Muslim's life. In Saudi Arabia, the government is not a constitutional one, but rather a monarchy. Legal judgments and jurisprudence are taken from the Holy Quran, the legal code which is called the Sharia. What this postulates is a conflict between our constitutional ideology, which includes the clear separation of church and state, and that of Islam, where no such distinction exists. We in the West fail to understand that Middle Eastern countries do not want our form of government or democracy. The Sharia within the Quran has existed for hundreds of years and it has served Islam very well.

Once Islam has been described as a pure and integrated

21

religion, the question arises: from where do Islamic Terrorism, Holy Terror, Jihad, or Holy War evolve? Before we enter the world of Jihad, let me further explain the word, 'fundamentalism'. Again, we are misled and misguided by the prejudice and lack of knowledge of the media, who use the word in every other headline or sentence when reporting on Middle East terrorist activity. Do we have Christian fundamentalists in the United States? Of course we do. Are they terrorists simply because they have an extreme ideology? No. In simple terms, fundamentalists espouse the return to a 'basic values' form of life under the Holy Quran. The more moderate Islamists consider themselves as undergoing a religious revolution, with social and economic ramifications, but there are aberrations to the theory of revival, and these account for the use of violence, or terrorism.

Islam, for the most part, is theologically and historically ingrained in the personality of Muslims. However, the qualities of Islam did not attract attention from the political world until the outbreak of the Islamic revolution in Iran and the accompanying escalation of violence by some Islamic groups throughout the Middle East. Having reflected on Islam as a pure and kind religion, it is only fair to note that Islam is not our adversary. Our adversary is the subjective interpretation by pseudo-political religious leaders who have utilized Islam to further their regional and international conflicts, and to foster a regimen of anti-Western rhetoric via this means they have perverted Islam.

The United States, in supporting regional Middle Eastern leaders through financial and military aid, has transgressed against the will of the majority of people of those countries who view their leaders as having abrogated their responsibility to Islam, thus becoming sinners. When American military troops are guests of various Middle Eastern governments, the populace resents this unlawful occupation, consequently resorting to the teaching of the Holy Quran in seeking redress for this invasion of corruption, and attack on Islam. The avenue taken is called Jihad, or Holy War.

However, before we explore the concept of Jihad, it is necessary to continue with our discussion of the ethos surrounding the Middle Easterner. To this end, the personality traits inherent in Middle Easterners will be identified in broad generic terms. The information has been culled from various writings, especially the works of Raphael Pati.[2] I will start with what are called basic Arab values.

Basic Arab Values
* A person's dignity, honor, and reputation are of paramount importance and no effort should be spared to protect them, especially one's honor.
* It is important to behave at all times in a way which will create a good impression on others.
* Loyalty to one's family takes precedence over personal needs.
* Social class and family background are the major determining factors of personal status, followed by individual character and achievement.

Basic Arab Religious Attitudes
* Everyone believes in God, acknowledges his power, and has a religious affiliation.
* Humans cannot control all events; some things depend on God (i.e. 'Fate').
* Piety is one of the most admirable characteristics in a person.
* There should be no separation between Church and State; religion should be taught in schools and promoted by governments.
* Religious tenets should not be subjected to 'liberal' interpretations or modifications which can threaten established beliefs and practices.

Basic Arab Self-perceptions

* Arabs are generous, humanitarian, polite and loyal. Several studies have demonstrated that Arabs see these traits as distinguishing them from other groups.

* Arabs have a rich cultural heritage. This is illustrated by their contributions to religion, philosophy, literature, medicine, architecture, art, mathematics, and the natural sciences.

* Although there are many differences among Arab countries, the Arabs are a clearly defined cultural group, members of the 'Arab Nation' (Al-Umma Al-'Arabiyya).

* The Arab people have been victimized and exploited by the West. For them, the experience of the Palestinians represents the most painful and obvious example.

* Indiscriminate imitation of Western culture, by weakening traditional family ties and social and religious values, will have a corrupting influence on Arab society.

* Arabs are misunderstood and wrongly characterized by most Westerners.

Arabs feel that they are often portrayed in the Western media as excessively wealthy, irrational, sensuous and violent, and there is little counterbalancing information about ordinary people who live family and work-centered lives on a modest scale. One observer has remarked, 'The Arabs remain one of the few ethnic groups who can still be slandered with impunity in America.'

The adult Arab makes statements which express threats, demands, or intentions which he does not intend to carry out, but which, once uttered, relax emotional tension, give psychological relief and, at the same time, reduce the pressure to engage in any act aimed at realizing the verbalized goal. Once the intention of doing something is verbalized, this verbal information itself leaves in the mind of the speaker the impression that he has done something about the issue at hand,

24

which in turn psychologically reduces the importance of following it up by actually translating the stated intention into action. There is no 'confusion between words and action, but rather a psychologically conditioned substitution of words for action.' The verbal statement of a threat or an intention (especially when it is uttered repeatedly and exaggeratedly) achieves such importance that the question of whether or not it is subsequently carried out becomes of minor significance.

Criticism
Arabs usually feel that criticism of their work, if it is phrased too bluntly, is a personal insult.

Intermediaries
The designation of one person to act as an intermediary between two other persons is very common in Arab society. Personal influence is very helpful in getting decisions made and things done, so people often ask someone with influence to represent them. (In Arabic, an intermediary is called a 'wasta'.) Mediation, or representation through a third party, also saves face in the event that a request is not granted, and it gives the petitioner confidence that maximum influence has been brought to bear.

Fatalism
Fatalism, or a belief that people are helpless to control events, is part of traditional Arab culture. It has been much overemphasized by Westerners, however, and is far more prevalent among traditional uneducated Arabs than it is among the educated elite today. It nevertheless still needs to be considered, since it will usually be encountered in one form or another by the West.

For Arabs, fatalism is based on the religious belief that God has direct and ultimate control of all that happens. If something goes wrong, a person can absolve himself of blame or justify doing nothing to make improvements or changes by assigning the cause to God's will. Indeed, too much self-confidence about controlling events is considered a sign of arrogance, tinged with blasphemy. The legacy of fatalism in Arab thought is most apparent in the oft heard and more or less ritual phrase 'Inshallah' (if God wills).

Western thought has essentially rejected fatalism.

Reality

The mistake people in one culture often make in dealing with another culture is to transfer their function to the other culture's functions. A political scientist, for example, one summer, went to the Middle East to do some research and to analyze Egyptian newspapers. When he came back, he said to me, 'But they are all just full of emotions. There is no data in these newspapers.' I said, 'What makes you think there should be?'

Persuasion

Arabs and Westerners place a different value on certain types of statements. This misunderstanding leads to decreased effectiveness in negotiation. Arabs respond much more readily to personalized arguments than to attempts to impose 'logical' conclusions. When trying to make a persuasive case in a discussion with Arabs, it is helpful to supplement a discussion with personal comments. Reference to mutual friendship, or emphasis on the effect which approval or disapproval of the action will have on other people, is very powerful.

In the Middle East, negotiation and persuasion have been developed into a fine art. Participants in negotiations enjoy long, spirited discussions, and are usually not in any hurry to conclude them. Speakers feel free to add to their points of argument by demonstrating their verbal cleverness, using their

26

personal charm, applying personal pressure, and engaging in personal appeals for consideration of their point of view.

The display of emotion also plays its part; indeed, one of the most commonly misunderstood aspects of Arab communication involves their 'display' of anger. Arabs are not usually as angry as they appear to Westerners. Raising their voice, repeating points, even pounding the table for emphasis may sound angry, but in the speaker's mind, indicate sincerity. A Westerner overhearing such a conversation (especially if it is in Arabic), may wrongly conclude that an argument is taking place. Emotion connotes deep and sincere concern for the outcome of the discussion. Negotiators can often miss the emotional dimension in their cross-cultural transactions with Arabs.

Sensitive Subjects

There are two subjects which Arabs favor in social conversation – religion and politics – and both can be risky.

Muslims enjoy discussing religion with non-Muslim Westerners because of their curiosity about Western religious beliefs and because they feel motivated to share information about Islam with friends as a favor to them. They are secure in their belief about the 'completeness' of Islam, since it is accepted as the third and final refinement of the two previously revealed religions, Judaism and Christianity. They like to teach about Islam, which eventually leads to the question: Why don't you consider conversion? A Westerner may feel uncomfortable and wonder how to give a gracious refusal. The simplest, most gracious and acceptable answer is to state an appreciation of the information and a respect for Islam as a religion. A refusal to convert is not offensive.

Arabs like to talk politics with Westerners and readily bring up controversial issues like the Palestine problem and the legacy of colonialism and imperialism. Yet they are not prepared for frank statements of disagreement with their positions on these questions or even inadvertent comments which sound negative or supportive of the opposing side of the argument. The safest response, if complete agreement is unavailable, is a confinement to platitudes and patience for the subject to change, expressing a concern for the victims of war and a hope for a lasting peace. A frank, two-sided discussion is usually not constructive if the subject is an emotional one. Arabs remember only the statements made in support of 'the other side.'

Inevitably, the sensitivity of a subject to an Arab is apparent by his evasion of a direct response. Such evasion should not be explored.

Body Language

All Arabs share a certain basic vocabulary of body language. They stand close together and frequently touch each other in a conversation, and they look each other in the eye constantly, instead of letting their gaze drift to the side.

Gestures

Arabs make liberal use of gestures when they talk, especially if they are enthusiastic about what they are saying. Hand and facial gestures are thus an important part of Arab communication, and an understanding of these gestures is important to a complete comprehension of the discussion.

Men use gestures more than women, and less-educated people use them more than the educated. Some of them are listed below:

1. Move the head slightly back and raise the eyebrows: No. Move the head back and chin upward: no. Move the chin back slightly and make a clicking sound with the tongue: no.

2. After shaking hands, place the right hand to the heart or chest: greeting with respect or sincerity.

3. Hold the right hand out, palm downward, and move it as if

scooping something away from you: go away.

4. Hold the right hand out, palm upward, and open and close the hand: come here.

5. Hold the right hand out, palm upward, then close the hand halfway and hold it: give it to me.

6. Hold the right hand out, palm downward, and move it up and down slowly: quiet down.

7. Hold the right hand out, palm upward, and touch the thumb and tips of fingers together, then move the hand up and down: calm down; be patient; slowly.

8. Hold the right forefinger up and move it from left to right quickly several times: no; never.

9. Hold the right hand out, palm downward, then quickly twist the hand to show the palm upward: what? why?

10. Make a fist with the right hand, keeping the thumb extended upward: Very good, I am winning. (This is a victory sign. You may have seen this gesture made by Yasser Arafat when talking to the press.)

Names

In many Western societies, one indication of the closeness of a personal relationship is the use of first names. In Arab society, the first name is used immediately, even if it is preceded by 'Miss', 'Mrs', or 'Mr.'

Arabs do not refer to people by their third or 'last' name. Arab names, for both men and women, consist of a first name (the person's own), their father's name and their paternal grandfather's name, followed by a family name (in countries where family names are used). In other words an Arab's name is simply a string of names listing ancestors on the father's side. It would be the same as if a Westerner's name were John (given name) Robert (his father) William (his grandfather) Jones.

Because names reflect genealogy on the father's side, women have masculine names after their first name. Some people include 'Ibn' (son of) or 'Bint' (daughter of) between the ancestral names. This practice is common in the Arabian peninsula; for example, Abdel-Aziz Ibn Saud (son of Saud), the founder of the Kingdom of Saudi Arabia. In North Africa, the word 'Ben' or 'Ould' is used to mean 'son of', and 'Bou' which means 'father of' is also a common element of a family.

1. If a name sounds Western (George, William, Mary), it marks a Christian.

2. If a name is that of a well-known figure in Islamic history (Mohammed, Bilal, Salah-Eddeen, Fatma, Ayesha), it marks a Muslim.

3. Most hyphenated names using 'Abdel-' are Muslim. The name means 'Servant (Slave) of God', and the second part is one of the attributes of God (Abdallah, 'Servant of Allah'); Abdel-Rahman, 'Servant of the Merciful'; Abdel-Karim, Servant of the Generous'. There are a few Christian names on this pattern (Abdel-Malak, 'Servant of the Angel'; Abdel-Massih, 'Servant of the Messiah'), but over 90 percent of the time, a person with this type of name is Muslim. Muslims list 99 attributes for God altogether (all-powerful, all knowing, compassionate, all wise, etc.), and most of these are currently in use as names.

4. Names containing the word 'Deen' (religion) are Muslim (Sharaf-Eddeen, 'The Honor of Religion'; Badr-Eddeen, 'The Moon of Religion'; Sayf-Eddeen, 'The Sword of Religion').

5. Most Arab names have a meaning, so many are simply descriptive adjectives (Aziz, 'Dear'; Said, 'Happy'; Amin, 'Faithful'; Hasan, 'Good'). Such descriptive names do not mark religion.

6. Names which are both Quranic and biblical (Ibrahim, 'Abraham'; Sulaiman, 'Solomon'; Daoud, 'David'; Yousef, 'Joseph') do not mark religion.

The older a woman becomes, the more status and power she accrues. Men owe great respect to their mothers all their lives, and most men make every effort to obey their mother's wishes, even her whims. All older women in a family are treated with deference. A woman who is the mother of sons gains even more status.

Muslim women veil their faces, wholly or partially, in conservative countries such as Saudi Arabia, Kuwait, the Arabian Gulf States, Yemen and Libya, and to some degree in Morocco, Algeria, and Tunisia (this varies, depending on a woman's age and social class). Veiling has continued in rural areas or in very conservative families in such countries as Syria, Lebanon, Jordan, Iraq, Iran, Afghanistan, and Pakistan. The Quran itself says nothing about veiling, although it does urge women to be modest in their dress. Veiling has always been a matter of local custom, not a religious requirement. Arab women wear clothing which is at least knee-length and partially sleeved and often cover their hair. The practice of wearing floor-length, fully sleeved clothing is increasing, not decreasing, even in modern cities like Cairo, the rest of Egypt, Amman, Jordan, because of the increased influence of Islamic fundamentalism.

Tradition-oriented Arab men and women do not view the social customs and restrictions as repressive, but as complimentary to the status and nature of women. They see the restrictions as providing protection for women so that they need not be subjected to the stress, competition, temptations, and possible indignities present in 'outside' society. Some, but not the New Age Arab women, feel satisfied that the present social system provides them with security, protections and respect.

Some women, however, view their situation otherwise, and have begun pressing for greater social, legal and personal freedom. There is a clear trend toward relaxing some of the restrictions which have regulated women's activities. It is important for an outsider to keep both points of view in mind when analyzing or discussing this subject.

Smoking

The overwhelming majority of Arab adults smoke, although women seldom smoke in public. Smoking is considered an integral part of adult behavior and it constitutes, to some extent, the expression of an individual's 'coming of age.' Arab men, in particular, view smoking as a right, not a privilege. It is not rare to see people disregarding 'No Smoking' signs in airplanes, waiting rooms, or elevators.

Rules of Etiquette

Listed here are some of the basic rules of etiquette in Arab culture.

It is important to sit properly. Slouching, draping the legs over the arm of a chair, or otherwise sitting carelessly when talking with someone communicates a lack of respect for that person. Legs are never crossed on top of a desk or table.

When eating with Arabs, especially when taking food from communal dishes, the left hand is not used. (The left hand is considered unclean.)

At a restaurant, Arabs will almost always insist on paying, especially if there are not many people in the party or if it is a business related occasion. Giving in graciously after a ritual gesture to pay and then returning the favor later, is an appropriate response.

Arabs have definite ideas about what constitutes proper masculine and feminine behavior and appearance. They do not approve of long hair on men or mannish dress and comportment of women.

Family disagreements and disputes in front of others or within hearing of others are avoided by Arabs.

Arabic people should not be photographed without their permission.

Staring at other people is not usually considered rude or an invasion of privacy by Arabs (especially when the object is a fascinating foreigner.) Moving away is the best defense.

When eating out with a large group of people where everyone is paying his share, it is best to let one person pay and reimburse him later. Arabs find the public calculation and division of a restaurant bill embarrassing.

Most Arabs do not like to touch or be in the presence of household animals, especially dogs. Pets are kept out of sight when Arab guests are present.

Family Loyalty and Obligations

Family loyalty and obligations take precedence over loyalty to friends or the demands of a job. Relatives are expected to help each other, including giving financial assistance if necessary.

Family affiliation provides security. It assures a person that he will never be entirely without resources, emotional or material. Only the most rash or foolhardy person would risk being censured or disowned by his family. Family support is indispensable in an unpredictable world; the family is a person's ultimate refuge.

Members of a family are expected to support each other in disputes with outsiders. Regardless of personal antipathy among relatives, they must defend each other's honor, counter criticism and display group cohesion.

Divorce

Most Arab Christians belong to denominations which do not permit divorce. Among Muslims, divorce is permitted and carefully regulated by religious law. A Muslim man may divorce his wife if he wishes, but he risks severe damage to his social image if he is arbitrary or hasty about his decision. A man can divorce his wife by pronouncing the formula of divorce ('I divorce you') in front of witnesses. If he says the formula once or twice, the couple can be reconciled; if he repeats it three times, it is binding.

Some Arab countries follow Islamic law entirely in matters of divorce; others have supplemented it. Laws pertaining to divorce have been widely discussed and changes are constantly being proposed. For example, the custody of children is theoretically determined by Islamic law. Children are to stay with their mother until they reach a certain age (approximately seven years for boys and nine years for girls, though it differs slightly among countries), and then they may go to their father. This shift is not always automatic, however, and may be ruled upon by a court of religious judges, according to the circumstances of the case.

The Quran and the Bible

Much of the content of the Quran is similar to the teachings and stories found in the Old and New Testaments of the Bible. Islamic doctrine accepts the previous revelations to biblical prophets as valid, but states, as the Bible does, that people continually strayed from these teachings. Correct guidance had to be repeated through different prophets, one after the other. By the seventh century, doctrines and practices again had to be corrected through the revelations to Mohamed, who is known as the last or 'Seal' of the prophets.

Courage

* Bravery – willingness to risk one's life for the benefit of one's group.
* Courage – the ability to stand physical pain and emotional stress so that no sound or facial expression betrays the trial one is undergoing.
* Training for adolescent boys – tests courage – arms are burned, lashings administered.
* Preliminary to marriage, with bride looking on – skin removed from male organ, testicle, inner thigh – no crying sound – song of joy.

Generosity
* Muslim duty is to give 2½ percent of one's wealth to the poor – one of the five pillars of the faith of Islam.
* A man is judged on how he treats his guests.

Group Cohesion
* Personality traits are in pairs: at the positive end is the value or trait which aids and abets group cohesion and survival at the negative end opposite. E.g. bravery – cowardice (not acceptable).
* Members must defend the group no matter the personal risk.

Conflict Resolution
* Method of resolving conflict (mediator).
* Honor is at stake – to give in or appear to move an inch is devastating to one's honor, self-respect, dignity; this includes taking the first step.
* Tradition of invective and proclivity for boasting and verbal exaggeration – any face to face encounter between adversaries will aggravate the dispute.

The West: Satan
Reasoning behind the hatred factor:
* Arabs contributed to the cultural development of the West – no sharing of technology.
* Muslims defeated great empires – emotional tie and dependence.
* Religion alone is not sufficient motivation for the hatred of the West.

The Fahlawi
* The most important psychological resource is the removal and relegation of responsibility from a person to others or by relegation to an area outside his own sphere. Motivation of this

personality trait is not dedication to duty nor a wish for self realization but rather the desire of reward or fear of punishment.

* Courage is external – a social act.
* Internal weakness is hidden behind the macho façade.
* Believes in himself and not aware of his internal weakness.
* Weakness does become manifest when challenged and a violent reaction is produced.

Shame

* A mirror between a person and his society.
* Shaming techniques are inculcated into the younger generation.

Character of Face

* Arab culture – outward appearance of honor.
* Code of acceptable behavior requires an Arab to go to great lengths to save face. Physical danger, personal discomfort.

Honor

* Serves to strengthen the group.
* Shameful behavior – disruptive, tending to impair, weaken or endanger the social aggregate.
* Examples of honor:
   * virility – number of sons;
   * certain types of work;
   * sword – defense;
   * injury to honor must be revenged;
   * cause the Arab ego to be inflated.
* Aspersion cast against an Arab's virility.

Arab Personality

* Majority follow Bedouin ethos.
* Muslim jurists legal decisions – rely on Bedouin precedents.

* Bedouins are a kin-based society – requires extreme self-sacrifice of one's identity for the sake of the common group.

Fahlawi Personality, by Dr Hamid Ammar, Egyptian sociologist
Fahlawi Persian – sharp-witted – clever.
* A ready adaptability – adjust behavior to a rapidly changing situation – identified by a readiness to express superficial agreement and fleeting amiability which is meant to conceal the situation and hide true feelings.
* Self-assertion manifests itself in an exaggerated assertion of the personality and the persistent tendency.
* Force both sides to stop the fighting without losing face.
* Mediator is paramount.
* Usually a member of a higher or different social class.
* In North Africa, the Marabouts Holy Men are appointed conflict resolvers.
* Open a door to the conflict to allow participants a gentleman's way out.

Conflict
Arabs behavior in:
* Lex Talionis – law of retaliation;
* Dam Butlub Dam – blood demands blood;
* blood feuds not limited to Middle East;
* accepted honorable expression of manliness;
* value of honor is greater than life;
* Japanese and Arab honor is similar – a man will kill himself to make statement or achieve a goal.

Use of Ethical or Ethnic Force
* Increase personal awareness of the adversary to modify his position through personal appeals – 'Do it for your father's sake.'

* Assumption is that the adversary is bound by his paternal and learned obligation to his kinsmen and elders.
* Conflict represents potential dishonor to the group.
* Never determine guilt or innocence.
* Mediate, don't arbitrate (Quran).
* Reverse for PLO – want self representation in mediation.

The Jihad

Non-Muslims typically have very little truthful information about Islam, this being the result of false reporting and conflicting reports from Western sources. Especially misunderstood is the concept of Jihad and its political and religious meaning. Since we have seen so many with terrorist groups identifying themselves as Jihad organizations, it is often thought that Jihad is only associated with violence, sanctioned by the Holy Quran. Nothing could be further from the truth. Jihad is not singular in concept, and it is not violence personified.

Jihad, it is reported, has been in the Arabic language from the beginning of recorded Arabic. The concept was revolutionized by the Prophet Mohammed. Prior to the involvement of the Prophet Mohammed, Jihad in earlier times was identified with 'struggle', or 'exertion.'

To understand terrorist groups adopting Jihad as a banner to arms it is necessary first to understand the ingredients of this concept. There are two significant variations of Jihad. One is the personal Jihad, the other Jihad is in defense of Islam.

There are many references in the Holy Quran to Jihad. These deal with the struggle of the Muslim community against non-believers. This was not a directive to take up arms but to put trust in Allah and the teachings of the Quran. This theory is supported by the following verse. 'With Allah is the decision, in the past and in the future: on that day believers rejoice, with the help of Allah. He helps whom he will, and he is exalted in might, most merciful.'[3] In essence what is being taught is that one should endure personal sacrifice and struggle in the name of Allah, who will reward one for his obedience to the teachings of the Quran.

Further exploration of the concepts of Jihad, the Quran and Sunnah involves the moral aspects of Jihad. These are concepts I have gleaned from the writings of Jamilah Kolocotronis in her book, *Islamic Jihad* and members of the Islamic community and religious leaders. In this book, she cites the following moral aspects of Jihad:

* There is an obligation to fight in the cause of Allah.
* There are rewards for fighting.
* There is a reward for martyrdom.
* There is divine aid against the enemy.
* There is criticism of the hypocrites.
* There is exemption from fighting.

According to the author, these 'categories refer to the spiritual and emotional status of the Muslim fighter or Mujahid, and that of the Muslim community of military Jihad.'[4]

There is, thus, a reference to fighting in the name of Allah. This divergence from the personal struggle to the political and religious struggle is the foundation of the ideology of Middle Eastern terrorist groups who utilize Jihad as the spring board and authority to wage a holy war against the infidels – the Western influences. This struggle is no longer limited to the individual, or wasted diplomatic rhetoric, but is for the perceived threat against the existence of the principals of Islam.

One of the worst diplomatic initiatives undertaken by the United States to date was the support of the Shah of Iran when the Iranian Revolution began to fester. Our government failed to understand the power of fundamentalist thinking and the influence of the Holy Quran. The spiritual teachings of the Ayatollah Ruhollah Khomeini transferred Islam into a modern day political–religious entity that has spawned an Islamic Revolution whose goals are worldwide domination.

The following are the words of the Ayahtollah Khomeini:
Islam is not a Religion of Pacifists

There are two kinds of war in Islam: one is called Jihad [Holy War], which means the conquest of [other] countries in accordance with certain conditions. The other [type] is war to preserve the independence of the [Muslim] country and to repel foreigners. Jihad or Holy War, which is for the conquest of [other] countries and kingdoms, becomes incumbent after the formation of the Islamic state in the presence of the Imam or in accordance with his command. Then Islam makes it incumbent on all adult males, provided they are not disabled and incapacitated, to prepare themselves for the conquest of [other] countries so that the writ of Islam is obeyed in every country in the world.

But world public opinion should know that Islamic conquest is not the same as conquests made by other rulers of the world. The latter want to conquer the world for their own personal profit, whereas Islam's conquest is aimed at serving the interests of the inhabitants of the globe as a whole. [Non-Islamic] conquerors want to rule the world so that they can spread through it every injustice and sexual indecency, whereas Islam wants to conquer the world in order to promote spiritual values, and to prepare mankind for justice and divine rule. [Non-Islamic] conquerors sacrifice the lives and possessions of the people to their own leisure and pleasure. But Islam does not allow its leaders and generals to enjoy themselves or to have a moment's leisure; in this way the lives and property of people can be protected and the bases of injustice destroyed in the world. Islam's Holy War is a struggle against idolatry, sexual deviation, plunder, repression and cruelty. The war waged by [non-Islamic] conquerors, however, aims at promoting lust and animal pleasures. They care not if whole countries are wiped out and many families left homeless. But those who study Islamic Holy War will understand why Islam wants to conquer the whole world. All the countries conquered by Islam or to be conquered in the future will be marked for everlasting salvation. For they shall live under Light Celestial Law. . .

Those who know nothing of Islam pretend that Islam counsels against war. Those [who say this] are witless. Islam says: Kill all the unbelievers just as they would kill you all! Does this mean that Muslims should sit back until they are devoured by [the unbelievers]? Islam says: Kill them [the non-Muslims], put them to the sword and scatter [their armies]. Does this mean sitting back until [non-Muslims] overcome us? Islam says: Kill in the service of Allah those who may want to kill you! Does this mean that we should surrender [to the enemy]? Islam says: Whatever good there is exists thanks to the sword and in the shadow of the sword! People cannot be made obedient except with the sword! The sword is the key to Paradise, which can be opened only for Holy Warriors!

There are hundreds of other [Quranic] psalms and Hadiths [sayings of the Prophet] urging Muslims to value war and to fight. Does all that mean that Islam is a religion that prevents men from waging war? I spit upon those foolish souls who make such a claim.[5]

The Ayatollah Khomeini seized power in Iran on February 11, 1979. The charismatic religious and political leader who was in exile managed to conduct a revolution right under the noses of the United States intelligence and security apparatus, unopposed. The intelligence and diplomatic failure of Western intelligence services opened the flood gates for Islamic revolutionary groups to thrive.

The above quotation from Khomeini is a clear message to the followers of the Islamic Revolution. It is obvious that the principles of Jihad defined by Khomeini were not taken seriously by intelligence services and world leaders, much to their discredit. The message contained in these writings has gained a dramatic influence over the everyday lives of Islamic revolutionaries – as evidenced by the survival of the Islamic Revolution after all these years. (I guess no one was listening!)

As a result of monumental intelligence and diplomatic failures, there were more than 380 US fatalities and close to 400 Americans injured in terrorist operations conducted under the banner of the Islamic Revolution, between 1983 and 1986. Also during this period some '570 attacks against American interests in the Middle East were committed by these Holy Terror squads.'[6]

The most desirable method of attack was the suicide car bomb. This method is well documented in the annals of various US government publications, including the US State Department's publications on international terrorism.

Suicide is not acceptable under the teachings of Islam, since it is a selfish act. However, for the glory of Allah, and continuance and defense of Islam, it has become a glorious act – a one way ticket to the Garden of Paradise.

The mindset of the Islamic warrior and his willingness to die for Islam is set forth in the following last will and testament, *'The Day Divine Light Opened My Eyes.'*[7]

In the Name of Allah the Avenger! Respected Mother, Exalted Imam,[8]

I address this, my last will, to both of you for a simple reason: it was my mother who brought me into this world so

42

that the Imam can show me the path to a better world – the path of martyrdom. To my mother I owe my earthly life, a most humble offering to the cause of the Imam. For what am I? A mere speck of dust in a whirlwind, shoved this way and that and never knowing why. This was my state so long as my eyes were closed with the leaden weight of dark ignorance. I thought life meant only growing up, going through an education, finding a mate and founding a family – a life of work and of repose. I knew not that my foolish concept of life had been inculcated in me by the vicious propaganda of those enemies of Islam whose corrupt culture of Cross-worship has dominated and polluted our land for too long. They want us [i.e., the Muslims] to throw off our guard, to relax, to begin to live life above everything else, to believe that happiness in this world is all that man requires. They try to seduce us with schools and houses so that we abandon our Faith and become like them, so that our womenfolk become prostitutes and our youth corrupted by sexual pleasure. Once our never-forgotten Guide Imam Musa Sadr had opened our eyes in this land of darkness, they [the Christians?] made him stay away from us in the hope that the fire he had lit would soon be put out by the passage of time and the intrigues of the enemies of Islam. But the Almighty was vigilant. For He had noticed our keen desire to be saved, our disdain for a restful life and our hatred of corruption of all kinds, whether of money or of a sexual nature. It was thus that the light of Imam Khomeini– may Allah never allow his enemies to have peace–began to shine on this lost and forgotten country. The youth of Lebanon discovered the Party of Allah and learned the sweet name of Khomeini – a name whose sweetness burns the tongue and warms the heart of every true believer. We learned to cry out: 'Allah is the One, Khomeini is the Guide!' And from then on Lebanon was

43

ours, the world was ours so that we could spit on it with disdain – we who seek another world. We saw the Light. We learned that Allah will always reserve His triumph for the downtrodden. We saw how He took our trembling hands and commanded us: 'Shi'ites of the south, of Sur and of Sidon and of the Jabal, stand up and fight!' I stood up and began to walk for the first time. Only then did I realize that throughout the previous twenty years of my life I had only crawled. I had crawled in the filth of humiliation. I had claimed to be a Shi'ite, that is to say a follower of Ali, the everlasting symbol of manly courage. And yet I had been a coward. I had watched as the party of Satan conquered my land to make our boys wear indecent clothes and behave like girls and to teach our women folk to lust after superficial things and carnal joy. They [the unbelievers?] taught us to drink wine so that we would forget the blood of Hussein, the Lord of Martyrs. We were turned into walking piles of filth and did not deserve a second look. And yet, Khomeini showed us the path. He spoke the will of Allah, and those who had the good fortune to hear his voice first were taken away from the dirt of this world and led to the gate of the garden whose key is martyrdom. I am at the door now, and praise and thank the Almighty for my good fortune. I am seeking the key to the gate of the garden. And I pray day and night to be allowed to feel the key in my hand, to be allowed to hear the key turn in the lock of the garden gate. And then to enter the garden, to see its wonders. The Imam has commanded me to kill. I shall kill for him. The Imam has commanded me to die. I shall die for him. I may be taken away at any moment. I pray constantly to be taken away at any moment – fighting sword in hand in the service of Allah, as were the companions of Hussein in the Karbala desert.[9] All I ask for is that my little Safwan[10] be brought up in the tradition of martyrdom from the earliest age, so that he does not waste as many years as I wasted. This trust I bequeath to my mother and friends and all others who have had the good fortune to become members of the Party of Allah. . .

The determination and resolve of the Islamic warrior to die for Islam are demonstrated in the above *'last will and testament.'* The adoption of this mindset ingrains an identity within the group, garnished with the ultimate goal of dying for Islam; no greater deed need be accomplished. The mixture of self-serving interpretations of Islam by political–religious leaders and the readiness for the ultimate sacrifice in a Mujahedeen soldier, in the name of Allah, creates a most formidable adversary. This volatile combination is an enigma to the conservative Western models of behavior which are taught in police academies. During my many years of lecturing throughout the United States in law enforcement circles, I endeavored to convince my fellow officers of their vulnerability with regard to this adversary. The adversary is not Islam, but the manipulation and use of Islam, in certain instances, to further a perceived cause. I was and still am astounded at the lack of intelligence operations to counter this perennial threat. The fundamentalist or revolutionary movement on behalf of Islam finds its foundation in student movements throughout the Middle East and American cities and universities. The recruits are young, have working minds, and have developed clandestine operating cells through the years.

In other words, we have been told for years what our adversary is thinking, what his goals are; our opponents have shown their operational capability over time. Once again, no one was listening, and if they were, they were miscalculating the enormity of the threat and the resolve to accomplish the task. The fundamentalist ideology is to protect Islam from taking Western ideals and poison in what it perceives as the unfair support of Israel against the Palestinians, the hypocritical human rights propaganda, and support for phony Islamic leaders; and to get out of this, the fundamentalists believe, the US will be put to the sword of Allah. And so it was when the Islamic terrorists bombed the World Trade Center, the largest symbol of arrogance and world power.

'The Art of War teaches us to rely not on the likelihood of the enemy's not coming, but on our own readiness to receive him, not on the chance of his not attacking, but rather on the fact that we have made our position unassailable.'[11]

Since the Islamic Revolutionaries consider themselves at war with the West and in particular the United States, their tactics, including terrorism, are considered justified under their rules of engagement. The insurgents have told us, the West, what their plans are, and how they plan to achieve their goals.

The Port Authority's Attempt to Identify the Adversary

The Port Authority recognized that there was a viable threat against its vast infrastructure. The organization began to take steps to alleviate its vulnerability and the attractiveness of its targets by employing various security disciplines to examine the weaknesses. The initial stage was my developing the terrorist intelligence operational data base and a program consisting of target identification at various commands. Born out of my efforts and lack of institutional support was the Office for Special Planning.

The basic approach was to identify targets within each facility that would fall into two categories: critical targets and non-critical targets. Critical targets are those targets which, if attacked, would cause extreme damage and greatly reduce the facility's operational capacity. Non-critical targets, if attacked, would be damaged, but would be able to function and there would be minimal impact on the overall operation of the facility.

These concepts were not too difficult to grasp and provided a clear delineation of vulnerability and recoupability. Since terrorists at the time targeted transportation facilities most of the time, and since vehicle bombs were the weapon of choice, the vulnerability of the World Trade Center, and specifically its garage, to terrorist attack, was high. They knew it and ignored it!

The World Trade Center, not only symbolic in name, was perceived to represent the arrogance of the United States. There were some forty foreign entities located at the complex, including an economic office of the Israeli Government.

Developing a strategy to mitigate potential terrorist activity requires at least two important ingredients: intelligence gathering and the existence of good physical security measures. Both of these concepts must work in tandem in order to effect the highest level of protection. If there is an intelligence or information failure, as in the case of the World Trade Center bombing, then it is critical that the physical security measures in place be able to deter, deflect, and defeat the potential attack. The target must be 'hardened' to the extent that external insurgent forces or terrorists are deterred. The failure to harden the World Trade Center, especially its critical areas, increased its vulnerability, and made it a more attractive target.

Once a critical area has been defined with respect to its importance to the overall operational capability of the target, that component must be protected.

When one institutes a security program, the program must be goal-oriented. While protecting against the highest threat level, i.e. terrorism, the security system implemented should also address the normal security concerns, such as criminal activity, theft and other associated criminal behavior.

The ultimate goal in target-hardening is to deny entry to hostile forces, to deter any potential attack, and to deflect the group away from its primary target. The failure by security planners to understand and implement this format will result in disaster. This is precisely what happened at the World Trade Center!

Critical targets were identified by in-house experts, the terrorist intelligence unit, the Special Planning Unit, and well-paid consultants. Unqualified debaters within the management structure of the Port Authority caused an already fragmented security system to develop a window of opportunity for terrorists to walk in and announce themselves. Approximately ten years earlier, I wrote a white paper outlining the security lapses at the World Trade Center, especially highlighting the critical security problem with regard to the sub-grade levels and recommending all security concerns be placed under the police commanding officer at the complex, to better facilitate and manage the security program. Again there was no response.

Intelligence
Having previously identified intelligence as one of the primary functional operational components of a security system, we wonder, considering all of the United States intelligence gathering and analysis capability, how the World Trade Center could be bombed.

I have had the opportunity and honor to participate with both the New York and New Jersey Joint FBI Terrorist Task Forces, and other intelligence gathering entities. I hold my fellow law enforcement colleagues in the highest regard for their dedication and professionalism. I have had many exciting and often hair raising experiences during my career, regretting none.

However, in the case of the World Trade Center bombing, there was a complete breakdown in the intelligence process. The inability of the agencies involved to understand the Middle Eastern mindset in tandem with the Islamic Revolution contributed to the success of the bombers. Traditional intelligence gathering methods, human and electronic were in place. The adversary was underestimated; the threat analysis made, but the Port Authority's indifference was overwhelming and fatalistic.

The Islamic Revolution did not commence with the World Trade Center bombing. It had been in place for centuries. However, the increased threat to the United States proper became more relevant with the November 1990 assassination of the radical Rabbi Meir Khane. The arrest of El Sayyid Nosair, a thirty-four year old Egyptian immigrant, appeared to be the end of an isolated incident. Nosair was a graduate of Abu Nidal 'University of Guerrilla Warfare' and his ultimate goal was underestimated by the investigating agencies. The investigators seized boxes of information, some of it written in Arabic, including terrorist training instructions and bomb-making instructions. Included in the potpourri of intelligence was a future target hit list. The chief of detectives for New York City, Joseph Borelli, argued that this was an open and shut case and dismissed any other theories, including the terrorist conspiracy theory. Unfortunately for him, the FBI did not tell him of the volumes of material seized from Nosair's home. The prosecutor in the State's case was also shut out by the FBI's refusal to turn over the material. One would think the FBI would immediately transcribe the information and conduct an intelligence analysis regarding the contents. Instead, it sat in the evidence room until after the World Trade Center bombing.

The second blunder was the mishandling of the FBI's primary informant, Emad Salem, who was in the inner circle of Sheik Abdel Rahman and his gang of terrorists. Emad had told the FBI handlers that the group was preparing for an all out Holy War against American targets. His revelations were ignored. Continuing with the saga, the FBI made a classic mistake by assigning a female agent to control a Muslim informant. This showed cultural ignorance. The FBI began to complain about the miserable US$500 a week Emad was being paid. FBI superiors attempted to scapegoat the agent in charge for ineptitude, lack of foresight and botched terrorist investigation. Initially, the FBI had released Salem, only to eat crow and reinstate him after the fact.

The third blunder was the discontinuance of the surveillance of individuals weeks before the bombing. This decision was based on the lack of results from the surveillance. There was a man inside informing of a plot to blow up New York City targets. The potential terrorists should have been placed under twenty-four-hour surveillance.

Other contributory blunders by the investigative and intelligence community were the failure to detect and apprehend Ramzi Yousef as he slipped into the country. The State Department also allowed Sheik Abdel Rahman entry into the United States even though he was on the terrorist watch list.

There were other mistakes made as well. However, the vital fact is that intelligence failed to detect and discover in time an imminent and disastrous terrorist attack.

There is no question that an intelligence failure can be catastrophic to a security plan. Most assessments of a group's capability are based on past actions and tactics. This alone cannot provide the kaleidoscope of information for proper assessment. Investigation into training, support apparatus, finances, logistics and international support must be constantly pursued. The security plan implemented must be able to deny the group the ability to collect site intelligence and vital target information. This action forces the group to expend resources beyond their capability, thus making the target less attractive. By increasing the difficulty of access to the target, the target's risk is increased, thus forcing the group to weigh the value of the target versus the risk. Statistics show that in pre-attack planning there has to be a 90 percent probability of completing the attack effectively. The key here is to deny the group critical intelligence and deflect the attack. Even the most hapless of groups will not attack a target without critical tactical and target information.

It is clear that with the World Trade Center incident, data collection and site intelligence were not prevented by the existing security program. Access to the subgrade of the complex was easily accomplished without security interdiction or detection. Terrorist attacks are not random, nor is target selection. The Port Authority was well aware of the vulnerability of its facilities to terrorist attack. Their knowledge of the World Trade Center's vulnerability came directly from information passed on by my terrorist intelligence unit and the identification of critical infrastructure targets by the Office of Special Planning, which was established to identify critical targets and make appropriate recommendations.

The maxim that a terrorist will accomplish his task regardless of the risk and is willing to die for his beliefs is true, as in the case of suicide bombers. However, a security program which leaves the door unlocked and open does not need an extreme suicide bomber. A rented van with 1,500 pounds of explosives and approximately twenty feet of a fuse which could be manually lit, would do the trick, and it did.[12]

CHAPTER 4
The Seeds of Discontent

The radicalization of Islam and transfer of its ideology into action on US soil was not a kneejerk reaction by a handful of extremists. An examination of the history surrounding the development of extreme radical Islam in the United States starts with the Afghan insurrection against Russian occupation.

The US government, in its haste to confront communism in Afghanistan, contributed to the development of radical Islam. The United States supported the Mujahdeen Freedom Fighters, also known as Holy Warriors, through various foreign intelligence services. According to the Central Intelligence Agency we provided training, resources, covert operational capability, and munitions to the Holy Warriors fighting in Afghanistan against the Russian superpower. Traditional use of a surrogate in this instance was the Pakistani intelligence service. Using the surrogate, we funneled approximately US$3 billion to the Afghan Freedom Fighters to meet and ultimately defeat the communist threat. The reward for our involvement was the energizing of Islamic insurgents. Once the Soviets were defeated, the Islamic radicals adopted a confident posture that they could achieve victory against a superpower, and this formed a strong foundation for the basis of Jihad against the West. This position, concurrent with the Iranian Revolution, spawned several anti-Western Islamic radical organizations.

The Central Intelligence Agency failed to perceive a developing threat from these extremist organizations. It is apparent that the ideology behind anti-western rhetoric was viewed as being regional with no global expansion properties. This, I believe, allowed the development of radical Islamic ideology against internal and external governments to go unabated. This judgment is supported by hearings and reports showing that since the fall of 1992 there has been an increase of terrorist incidents attributed to Islamic radicals in India, Pakistan, Israel, Egypt, Jordan, Algeria, Nigeria, and Somalia.[13]

The focus of these groups, that is, the establishment of a religious government and society based on strict interpretations of the Holy Quran, was becoming clearly evident by the increase in violent activity by these groups. Intelligence reports show that in Cairo, Egypt, on February 26, 1993, the same day as the World Trade Center bombing, multiple terrorist attacks occurred. Just two weeks before the World Trade Center bombing, the Islamic Salvation Front attempted to assassinate the Algerian Defense Minister. On February 28, 1993, a bomb exploded at the Zamboanga Airport in the Philippines. Another event worthy of mention was the January 25, 1993, shooting that took place outside the Central Intelligence Agency, where two CIA employees were shot and killed by Mir Aimal Kansi, using an AK47 assault rifle. Kansi then fled to Afghanistan.

Analysis of these incidents points to Islamic radicals associated with groups such as Hamas, Hezbollah-Al-Jihad, the PLO and other terrorist organizations.[14]

The Islamic Revolution and its announced goals of world expansion are nothing new to the West. Nor is the centralized violence adopted by certain groups for the furtherance of 'the cause'. The inherent nature of these groups prevents any viable penetration or counter-terrorist campaign that is focused towards the neutralization of the 'threat.' There are many groups operating under various Islamic Jihad banners. This is unlike 'state sponsored terrorism,' where intelligence sources can track governments who support this activity.

The World Trade Center bombers were guided by, or under the religious and spiritual aura of, Sheik Abdul Rahman. This radical Egyptian cleric was exiled from Egypt for his complicity in the assassination of Egyptian President Anwar Sadat in 1984. This cleric's violent messages created the cohesiveness which allowed the conspirators in the World Trade Center bombing to hold together.

Ahmad Mohammad Aja was born in Palestine. He was arrested at Kennedy Airport illegally entering the country on a bogus passport. He was also found to be in possession of bomb-making manuals. He was identified as a member of the Palestinian group Fatah.

Ramsi Yousef arrived on the same flight from Pakistan as did Ahmad Aja, with a fraudulent passport. He worshipped at the mosque where Sheik Abdul Rahman preached. He fled the country after the bombing but was finally apprehended.

El Sayyid Nosair who is of Egyptian descent was acquitted of the 1990 slaying of radical Rabbi Meir Kahane but ultimately put away on associated charges. Prison visitor records show he was visited by Salameh and Abohalima before the bombing. Sheik Rahman was Nosair's spiritual leader. When law enforcement searched Nosair's house, they found detailed bomb making information, and targeting lists, but they failed to understand the significance of the information until after the bombing.

Mohammed Abouhalima was a cab driver in Brooklyn, New York. He was born in Egypt and a very active member of Sheik Rahman's organization, including acting as his driver. Mahmoud had fought with the Afghanistan resistance movement against the Russians, supported by United States aid and training. He was also suspected of being the driver of the getaway car at the Kahane slaying. He was captured in Egypt, tortured and returned to the United States. Detective Matt Besheer and I, along with other task force members, met Abouhalima upon his return from Egypt in the custody of Federal agents and we were part of his return escort. This terrorist was very happy to be back on US soil after a couple of days in an Egyptian interrogation room.

Mohammad Salameh was born in Palestine and has Jordanian citizenship. He entered the US on a tourist visa in 1988 and forgot to return home. He was a pivotal member of the conspiracy. Mohammad Salameh rented the van used in the World Trade Center bombing. He then returned to obtain his deposit, claiming the van had been stolen.

Ibrahim A. Elgabrowny was indeed a shoddy character. When the Terrorist Task Force raided his apartment in Brooklyn, Elgabrowny resisted arrest by the Task Force agents. He actually struck a Federal agent. In the apartment, the agents found an A9mm handgun and a phony passport for his cousin Nosair. The passports were of Nicaraguan origin, further indicating the expansiveness of the group's capability. The Sandinistas who were in control in Nicaragua at this time were very sympathetic to the Arab and Palestinian cause, hence the connection to the passports via the Nicaraguan immigration authorities.

Sheik Abdel Rahman's message to the flock was most provocative. 'Hit hard and kill the enemies of God in every spot to rid it of the descendants of apes and pigs fed at the tables of Zionism, Communism and Imperialism.'[15] Such sermons were the ideological foundation for action by his followers. His words were translated into action. 'The Sheik was trained at Cairo's Al-Azhar University and taught in both Egypt and Saudi Arabia.'[16]

The bombing of the World Trade Center was an act by a decentralized group of Islamic terrorists and, presumably, without the signature of highly disciplined cells like those which have permeated the world in the past. For the most part, there is little evidence of state sponsorship, although there are numerous suggested theories of Iranian or Iraqi support.

Nevertheless, the bombers took unnecessary risks. They gave their correct names and addresses when renting the van used in the bombing. The bomb was constructed in a rented storage locker, called the Space Station, in Jersey City, New Jersey. On March 5, 1993, the FBI raided the locker and recovered volatile bomb making materials. In the Federal complaint, FBI Special Agent Thomas Donlon stated that a forensic chemist in the Bureau of Alcohol, Tobacco and Firearms determined that the items seized could be combined to produce a 'high explosive.' The FBI, it is reported, found and removed 'several 100 pound bags labeled 'Urea,' and numerous bottles labeled 'nitric acid;' one plastic container labeled 'sulphuric acid;' numerous other chemicals and compounds; a pyrotechnic fuse; tubing; graduated cylinders; flasks; beakers; filter paper; funnels; a mortar and pestle and stirring rods.' The name Mohammad Salameh, the first suspect arrested in the World Trade Center bombing, appeared on the rental agreement.[17]

Although the bomb did the job, a highly trained sophisticated terrorist cell would probably have used a commercial or military plastic explosive such as SEMTEX or C-4. Further evidence of ineptitude in conducting a low intensity covert operation is reflected in the terrorists' failure to dead-end their telephone conversations. For instance, Salameh made telephone calls to the chemical engineer Nidal Ayyad from the storage locker. When arrested, Salameh had Nidal Ayyad's business card in his pocket.

On February 13, 1993, according to prison records, Salameh visited Nosair at Attica prison. This visit violated all known protocols regarding the methodology utilized by highly trained operatives. Investigation show two elements which cast doubts as to the independence of the terrorist cell responsible for blowing up the World Trade Center.

The first instance was the arrest of Ahmed Mohammed Aja when he was detained by US Immigration authorities at John F. Kennedy International Airport for being in possession of books and videos describing how to mix chemicals and instructions on how to make bombs. On the same flight from Pakistan was terrorist Ramzi Yousef, carrying a fraudulent Iraqi passport. He was not detained. Yousef, utilizing the name Abdul Basit, departed John F. Kennedy International Airport the evening of the bombing on a Pakistani flight for Karachi. Intelligence revealed that Aja was of Palestinian heritage, born in Jerusalem and a member of the Palestinian Terrorist organization Fatah. Ramzi Yousef was born in Kuwait, of Pakistani parents. It is reported he attended school in the United Kingdom and studied electronic engineering. Were these two individuals the catalysts to put the sleeper cell together? Whom did they receive their instructions from? Was it Iran, Iraq, the Afghanistan Islamic Jihad? What Islamic regime supported the operation? These questions have never been answered.

The second contributing element as to independent operation of the terrorist cell involves finances. Investigation exposed a number of wire transfers from Germany to banks in New Jersey, over time. According to German authorities, two money transfers were made to Nidal Ayyad's and Salameh's joint account at the National Westminster Bank in Jersey City. It is further reported that a 'relative of Salameh' wired US$2,400 into his bank account for injuries suffered in an earlier car accident. A subsequent wire transfer of funds was unearthed by the FBI investigation. Nidal Ayyad received US$40,000 through the Bank of Kuwait to his Morristown Federal Credit Union account in Morristown, New Jersey in October 1992.

Germany has been host to many Islamic radical organizations for many years. Groups from Iran, Pakistan, Afghanistan, and the Palestinian Liberation Organization have utilized Germany for trans-operational logistics. Was there direction from an outside source, or did this cell of Islamic terrorist act on the wisdom and spiritual guidance of Sheik Abdel Rahman? The answer is the conundrum.

My office at the Port Authority Police Headquarters was on the sixth floor. I had a clear view of Kennedy Boulevard in Jersey City and could view with binoculars the Al-Salam Mosque. During my lunchtime I would walk down to the mosque and observe the street activity. Every once in a while I would eyeball the law enforcement surveillance team in place near the mosque and chuckle. Blond white males really were not as covert as they thought, actually! I called the Task Force one day to alert them that their surveillance team was the topic of discussion by Middle Easterners on the street only to have the supervising agent brush me off. Nevertheless the Mosque was the center for the Gamma Al-Islamiya (Islamic group) to meet and hear the words of their spiritual leader Sheik Abel Rahman. The Islamic group was an offshoot of the Muslim Brotherhood founded in Egypt by Hassan Al Banna in the 1920s to rid the area of the dominance of the British Empire. They became a very powerful and political movement, with members like Anwar Sadat and Gamel Abdel Nasser, later Presidents of Egypt. The ideology of the Jihad movement can be found in the writings of Abd Salam Faraj, a colleague of Sheik Rahman. Faraj, it is reported, circulated a pamphlet in the 1980s in Egypt called 'The Neglected Duty.' He urged war against the enemies of Islam and legitimized the use of terrorism. He argued that the Holy Quran and other religious doctrines define fighting as shedding blood for Islam. He further stated that it is the duty of Muslims to participate in Jihad and that Muslims who adopt the Western culture are subject to a Fatwah. Faraj could not save his own Islamic self; he was executed in 1982 for his part in the Anwar Sadat assassination.

Both of these radical clerics obtained their ideology from the spirited writings of another Islamic writer. In the 1950s, after spending time in the United States studying educational administration, Sayid Qutb asserted in *This Religion of Islam* that

Muslims should return to the basic values of Islam because the West was corrupting family and political values in a way that was contrary to the teachings of the Holy Quran. Qutb too was executed for his role in political assassinations. A man can be killed, but his thoughts will live in perpetuity. In this case, some forty years later, Jihad against Western values were not only planted, but grew.

CHAPTER 5
The Perpetrators

Sheik Abdel Rahman was described as the spiritual leader of
Hamas. At the time of the World Trade Center bombing very
little was known about this group outside classified intelligence
circles. The full Arabic name is Harakatu I-Mujawamati I-
Islamiya, Islamic Resistance Movement. The group evolved
around 1988 from elements of the Muslim Brotherhood, which
was active in the West Bank with religious and educational
work. The relationship between the two groups was very good,
making them virtually identical with each other. The group
developed prominence with the support of the Intifada, or
better known as the Palestinian Public Resistance.

Ahmad Rashad wrote a complete account of Hamas called
'The Truth About Hamas: Palestinian Politics with an Islamic
Hue.' The following pages contain the full text explaining the
history of Hamas, including the group's political position.

Upon reading the document written by Ahmad Rashad,
several interesting analytical thoughts come to mind. For
instance, Sheik Abdel Rahman is not mentioned as a spiritual
leader of the group. Second, the focus of Hamas' political
agenda was not to give up Palestinian land to the Israelis. The
group's target was the Israeli Defense Forces using the 'Izzedin
Qassam Brigades' commando units. Their directive was to
operate directly within the occupied territories. Several leaders
of Hamas met with Western diplomats, including US diplomats,
towards the end of 1991. The US State Department placed the
group on the Terrorist Watch List by including it in an annual
report on global terrorism. Interestingly, Israeli intelligence
allegedly warned the United States that Hamas was operating

on US soil. Several US legislators supported investigations into this group. The FBI confirmed that Hamas was conducting fund raising within the United States and made some arrests. Were any full blown conspiracy investigations conducted? Did anyone bother to read the Charter of Hamas?

The Charter of Hamas is replete with information and insight into the political and ideological makeup of the group. Were the World Trade Center bombers members of Hamas? It is possible. Sheik Abdel Rahman, who is Egyptian, was never acknowledged by the original leader of Hamas, Sheik Ahmed Yassin, after his release from an Israeli prison.

Regardless of the lack of public pronouncement, Hamas was a group with the vision and capacity to blow up the World Trade Center.

The Truth About Hamas (**Ahmad Rashad's words**)
Introduction

"Despite its relative youth, Hamas, has become a significant force in the realm of Palestinian politics. A number of factors have led to its growing grass-roots popularity: its call for the liberation of all Palestine; a reputation for efficiency, honesty and lack of corruption; daring and successful attacks on Israel military targets; a remarkable resilience to Israel crackdowns; the presence of its leadership largely within the territories, as opposed to the PLO's expatriate direction; and its firm yet pragmatic approach to a nationalist camp seen increasingly as abandoning the armed struggle against the 'Zionist entity'.

The movement's ability not only to survive thus far, but to present itself as a significant contender for the mantle of Palestinian representation, comes from a combination of its populism and a prudent approach to inter-Arab affairs that affect support for its operations. The recent peace accord is not likely to deter Hamas' policy of confronting the

61

occupation. The Islamists view the agreement as a superficial document aimed at legitimizing Israel control of Palestinian land and resources. They have expressed concern over the possibility of bloody inter-factional violence. They have repeatedly issued leaflets forbidding members from engaging in such acts. Hamas' pragmatism has ensured its longevity; it will remain an important element in the future of the occupied territories.

Initially, Hamas identified itself as a wing of the Palestinian Muslim Brotherhood (MB). The strong affinity stems from the fact that several Brotherhood cadres were instrumental in Hamas' establishment.

The Brotherhood had been priming a political wing, albeit a vague one, for some time prior to the uprising. It decided, during 1985/86, to implement a policy of resistance through civil disturbance. It issued leaflets to this effect under several names, such as Harakat al-Kifah al-Musallh (Armed Struggle Movement), al-Murabitoon ala Ard al-Isrá (The Steadfast on the Land of al-Isrá), and Harakat al-Muqawama al-Islamiyya (Islamic Resistance Movement, IRM). These communiqués were concerned primarily with corruption and immorality; but they became more politicized as tensions escalated in the territories. The IRM distributed leaflets during 1987 warning Palestinians against the tactics employed by the Shin Bet, Israel's secret service, of using intimidation, drugs, blackmail, and sexual coercion to induce young Palestinians to collaborate against activities. 'Hamas' began appearing on the IRM communiqués during January 1988.

Structure

Hamas is composed of administrative, charitable, political, and military elements, each of which has subdivisions. The administrative wing coordinates the movement's actions.

Charity work is conducted in cooperation with other Islamic centers sympathetic to Hamas. The political activity that takes place within the territories is confined to Hamas sympathizers participating in local elections. The 'military' wing is the most active within the occupied territories, particularly since Hamas' main goal is combatting the Israeli occupation.

Given that all the founders were Brethren, Hamas' structure borrows heavily from the movement. For example, each region is comprised of 'families' and branches, answerable to an administrative center. There is more than one kind of Hamas member. The four general categories into which they fall are: intelligentsia, sheiks (religious leaders), younger leadership candidates, and activists.

Hamas was designed to allow for the induction of members not affiliated with the Brotherhood. Several elements of the Brethren that were transferred to Hamas were eventually phased out and replaced by similar cells that remain highly secretive. Two examples are al-Majd and al-Mujahidün, established in 1983, the Brotherhood's intelligence and commando units, respectively. Israeli forces were able to crack down on these groups within the first two years of the intifada. They reemerged later as part of the 'Izzedin Qassam Brigades,' which function independently of Hamas' main operations.

The intelligence wing implements six directives: conduct surveillance of collaborators and drug dealers; castigate those found guilty of treason, prostitution or selling narcotics (punishment ranges from verbal warning to execution); distribute the group's 'information' leaflets; publicize Israeli recruitment policies for collaboration and warn the populace against complicity; write and distribute communiqués; and manage logistic support for the organization. The intelligence wing also monitors crime in the territories. Israeli occupation authorities ceased directing their resources toward combating crime at the intifada's outset. In fact, criminal activity is tolerated because it provides ample ground for the recruitment of informants.

The commando units have four primary objectives: establish usar (families) and underground cells; gather information on the Israeli Defence Force (IDF) activities, for use in planned operations; conduct training sessions in hand-to-hand combat; and carry out military operations, including the abduction of enemy soldiers. These two groups operate exclusively within the occupied territories and Israel. Hamas founders created other wings that are in constant contact with the inside, but fulfill their functions outside. These are al-Maktab al-I'lami and al-Maktab al-Siyassi, the Information and Political Offices, respectively.

The Information Office, located in Jordan, is responsible for preparing and disseminating all press releases concerned with Hamas statements of policy. It also issues publications in Hamas' name. The Political Office is concerned with Hamas' foreign relations and represents the organization at conferences and meetings that deal with Palestinian affairs. These two appendages to the movement were borne out of the Gulf War, in order to maintain the movement's contact with foreign officials and journalists.

Goals

The Islamists first revealed a synopsis of their goals in a January 22, 1988 communiqué. Immediate objectives were: 'release of the detainees' rejection of the settlements, the policy of expulsion, administrative detention, brutalization of civilians and detainees, the denial of travel, harassment, the spread of immorality, bribery, corruption, entrapment in the nets of the secret service, the denial of the right of return, astronomical taxes, and other reprehensible occupation policies.' The group's charter would reinforce these aims, but would also keep the door open for political activity.

Hamas issued its long-term goals in April 1994. The movement declared that it is not opposed to the principle of peace. In addition, it outlined a pragmatic policy position by declaring its willingness to cease military operation in the West Bank and Gaza, as long as the following conditions are met: 1) complete Israeli withdrawal from the occupied territories; 2) disarm the settlers and dismantle the settlements; 3) place international forces on the 'green line' established in the occupied territories during the '48 and '67 wars; 4) free and general elections to determine true representation of the Palestinian people; and 5) the Council, which will be composed of electoral victors, shall represent the Palestinians in any negotiations that determine their future and that of the occupied territories.

Support and Funds

Relief centers operated predominantly by Islamists are sometimes given the distinction of being 'Hamas' institutions. While the reference is not completely incorrect, it is misleading. There are numerous Muslim activists who sympathize with Hamas but have limited knowledge about its operations. These activists are involved in eleemosynary foundations, development projects, health clinics, and so on. Some of them do provide either moral or material support to Hamas' political wing. This earns the institutions in which they work a 'Hamas' label. Some prominent commentators have pointed out the ambiguities involved. That there is a link between Hamas and these operations, however, is not in doubt. Put simply, Hamas works within the framework of Islamic institutions in the occupied territories, but not as a clearly defined organization as may be implied when discussing Hamas' social projects.

Nevertheless, the fact remains that most of Hamas' funds and efforts are directed toward assisting the populace. Sarah Roy, a visiting scholar at the Center for Middle Eastern Studies at Harvard University, notes:

Hamas runs the best social service network in the Gaza Strip. . . Structured and well organized, Hamas is trusted by the poor (Gaza's overwhelming majority) to deliver on its promises, and is perceived to be far less corrupt and subject to patronage than its secular nationalist counterparts, especially Fateh. Indeed, it is not only Palestinians who regard Hamas in this way, but a growing number of foreign assistance providers as well. Some senior officials at UNRWA [United Nations Relief Works and Agency] in Gaza acknowledged that Hamas is the only faction they trust to distribute UNRWA food donations to the people.

Pro-Hamas Islamists, in coordination with the Brethren, collect zakat (an obligatory 2.5 per cent of a Muslim's earnings) via local committees. These funds are used in helping the poor, building mosques and schools, and other charitable work. In addition to donations, Hamas supporters create small projects aimed at generating limited income but allowing self-sufficiency. These include the production of honey, cheese-making ventures, and home-based clothes manu-facturing. Finally, the Islamists allocate a considerable portion of their resources to assisting younger Palestinians.

The movement's funding is equally difficult to discern. Although a great deal has been written about an Iranian and/or Saudi connection, there has been little substantial evidence to corroborate such assertions. During the uprising's early days, journalists identified Hamas as 'a Saudi-backed Islamic group'. The P.L.O.'s Yasser Arafat has stated that Hamas received between $20 to $30 million from Iran, a sum repeated frequently in the media. Claiming that Hamas funds stem primarily from Tehran began during 1989, when Israel first decided that the group was a serious security threat, the P.L.O. jumped on the bandwagon. In reality, Hamas has shown no leanings toward a specific government in seeking support. Its spokesmen aver that most of its financial resources depend on philanthropic individuals and organizations. Among the groups that have extended assistance to Hamas are the international Muslim Brotherhood, Islamic organizations in the Indian continent, and Islamic factions in Turkey, Malaysia, and Afghanistan. According to Ibrahim Ghosheh, Hamas' official spokesman, 'the fact of the matter is that Hamas receives modest support from many Muslims in the Gulf states, Saudi Arabia, Iran, Jordan, Yemen, Turkey, and many others.'

Elections

Despite the presence of far richer P.L.O. institutions, Hamas has enjoyed tremendous support in the territories. The results of local elections provide an indication of popular support for Hamas. During June 1992, Palestinians in the West Bank city of Hebron held the first civil elections in the territories for 15 years; and Islamists sympathetic to Hamas won. Islamists defeated P.L.O. candidates in union elections at Al Makassed Hospital in East Jerusalem during the same period. When elections took place in Ramallah, a city with a large Palestinian Christian community, Hamas candidates beat the P.L.O. in an election for the board of the Chamber of Commerce.

Several months later Mahmoud al-Zahhar, a pediatrician and political activist sympathetic to the Islamists, conducted a study of election results for the Bar Association, the Engineers' Syndicate, the Medical Association, the Accountants Association, the Gaza Chamber of Commerce, and the UNRWA Workers' Union. According to al-Zahhar, 34,221 Palestinians voted in these elections and Islamist candidates won 43 per cent of the overall votes. Overall, however, Hamas won the majority of votes. In occupation, Hamas maintains combative underground cells.

Hamas and the PLO
Hamas' relationship to the P.L.O. is complex and precarious at best. The Islamists have neither, to date, wanted nor been able to alienate the nationalist camp. Their fates are intertwined, particularly since, prior to the intifada, a number of disillusioned Brethren had joined the P.L.O., and many current Islamists are former nationalists.

When the intifada began, fiery imams and younger members of Hamas set out to establish themselves as revolutionaries on a par with the nationalists. They did not view themselves as an alternative, although, privately, the leadership did not rule that out. Even when Islamists were deported to southern Lebanon, and the nationalists made only token objection, Islamic leaders did not want to see the P.L.O. collapse. When The Jerusalem Report asked the expellees' spokesman, Rantissi, if the P.L.O. financial crisis would strengthen Hamas, he responded: 'I would like to express a neutral voice, the voice of a Palestinian who does not necessarily work for Hamas. If the PLO had to collapse, I'd be very sad. It would have a negative effect on our cause and our rights. Also, speaking from a narrow factional perspective, I don't believe it is in Hamas' interest to see the downfall of the PLO.' The Islamists were convinced that national unity should not be undermined irrespective of ideological announcement, stating emphatically that 'national reconciliation is the solution.'

The September 1993 Gaza-Jericho agreement came as a shock and surprise to many activists. The elite P.L.O. hierarchy had decided to risk making an alliance with Israel in order, among other things, to eliminate the Islamic challenge to its authority. Haim Ramon, the Israeli health minister, declared: 'We are fully aware to the raise [sic] of power of the extremists, of the fundamentalism in the Gaza Strip; and we believe that together, the moderate parts of the Palestinians and the Government of Israel, together, will fight and can win the fight against the extremists.'

According to Danny Rubinstein, a commentator for Ha¢aretz, 'Arafat will be able to bribe his society' away from Hamas with money secured from international donors. The deal marked the first time Hamas made unrelenting attacks against Arafat as a traitor. It sarcastically referred to the accord as a flagitious deal, al-ittfaqiyyah al-¢Arafatiyyah (Arafat's agreement), between the PLO chairman and the leadership of the 'Zionist enemy.'

In addition, the Islamists foresee inter-Palestinian clashes resulting from the deal. Muhammed Nazzal, a senior Hamas spokesman in Jordan, asserts: 'We are ready for the worst possibilities, including cooperation between the Palestinian police, [operating] under the orders of Yasser Arafat, and the Israeli army and the Shin Bet to confront the Hamas combatants.' Nevertheless, Hamas continues to adopt a cordial tone toward the PLO and Fateh.

Hamas and the West
Hamas' first contact with the West was toward the end of 1991, when it held meetings with several European diplomats. After Israel's expulsion of Islamist sympathizers,

Hamas met with several Western officials, including diplomats from the United States, Britain, Italy, and Germany. The movement's leaders have long considered cordial, if not friendly, relations with the West, an important part of their political agenda. Hamas leaders were perturbed, though not altogether surprised, when the State Department officially included the group in its annual report on global terrorism. Hamas stated that Assistant Secretary of State for Near Eastern Affairs Edward Djerejian's explanation for the move was 'strange.'

The State Department's move coincided with Israeli allegations that Hamas has established a nerve center on US territory. The movement's leadership accused the American government of succumbing to pressure from pro-Israeli pacts.

Pressure from pro-Israeli lobbyists arguably swayed a number of Congressmen into initiating a witch-hunt for alleged Hamas activists. This drive grew in intensity when Israel arrested several Palestinian Americans and charged them with being part of Hamas' US network. The first initiative came from Representatives Charles E. Grassley and Frank R. Lautenberg, who began their campaign by applauding the State Department's decision. They felt, however, that not enough had been done, writing: 'we believe the [State Department's annual] report should include a thorough review of the organization's activities and operations including fund-raising in the United States.'

Other Members of Congress who jumped on the bandwagon were Peter Deutsch, R. James Saxton, Alcee L. Hastings, and Ileana Ros-Lehtinen, who 'introduced H.R. 1279, a bill to list members of Hamas as individuals engaged in terrorist activity and to bar them from entering the United States.' The four repeated Israeli claims that 'over the past several years, Hamas has been conducting operations from several locations in the United States. Israeli intelligence has reportedly raised concerns about the scope of Hamas' operations in the US, and the FBI has confirmed that Hamas has engaged in fund-raising activities in US cities.'

Yet by far the sharpest attack came from New York's Senator Alfonse D'Amato who repeated Israeli rhetoric almost verbatim: 'This radical Islamic fundamentalist group is based in the Gaza Strip but also operates in Judea and Samaria.' He continued: 'Within our midst, this expansive network is aiding Hamas in its terror and murder in Israel. Acting in the guise of simple fund-raising, groups in northern Virginia, Dallas, Detroit, Chicago, Tucson, and in my State of New York, are channelling large amounts of money back to Hamas in the Gaza Strip. . .'

Representatives Jim Saxton and Peter Deutsch represent another example of blatant reliance on Israeli information. They photocopied and distributed a report by the Israel Defense Force's Information Branch to Congress. The two Representatives sent an attached note making the assertion that 'Hamas . . . [is] no longer confined to the Middle East, but organized enough to strike downtown America.' Despite Hamas' repeated insistence that it had no interest in striking U.S. interests, the aforementioned politicians continued their efforts.

In spite of the ominous warnings issued by some politicians, American security services have found little or no evidence of clandestine activity. Despite the inclusion of Hamas in the State Department's annual report on global terrorism, neither the State Department nor the FBI has lent credence to claims by Israel, the media, or politicians that Hamas operates a base on US soil."

CHAPTER 6
My Investigative Background

Atlantic Avenue, Brooklyn has been the hub of Arab American activity since the late 1980s. The arriving new immigrants developed one of the largest Arab American communities in the new world.

My father was born in the United States, my mother arriving as a young woman from Beirut, Lebanon. Being raised in the Arab American community allowed me to remain in touch with my heritage and provided me with an opportunity to savor the historical and cultural diversity that was ever present. My early childhood years were racked with family controversy, my father skipped out on his responsibilities, and I had a quick right hand when it came to settling differences. My impulsive behavior found me before a Family Court judge in Brooklyn for punching a teacher who had struck me in the face for laughing in class. The judge decided I should go to school out of the city and I was placed at Greer School in Dutchess County, New York. The school was a sleepaway for children from broken homes who showed potential but needed guidance.

I spent the next five years there, coming home on weekends and holidays. The experience paved the way for learning independence and respect. During my off time we worked at the farm, milking cows, moving manure and planting saplings in the vast fields. I also learned to hunt, fish, backpack, and generally survive off the land if needed.

After the eighth grade, we were bussed to Millbrook High School for the remaining four grades. It was difficult to assimilate into the school atmosphere since we had the reputation of being 'thugs from the city.' It did not take long for us to become part of the school community. The catalyst was our athletic ability that was learned from jumping and running away from the cops and street warfare. We won several titles in football, basketball and baseball. I earned two Most Valuable Player awards for basketball and was named to the All County's starting team twice. I regretted graduation since I had developed relationships akin to having a second family. Some thirty-five years later, I still hunt the area and visit my former high school friends and their families as if it were yesterday.

Upon graduation, I was lost. I could not attend college although I had partial scholarships for basketball. A decent paying job was not to be had in the city. The Vietnam War was cooking and I was eligible for the draft. I finally convinced my mother to sign the papers allowing me to join the Air Force as a cook. I was only seventeen. This, I felt, unrealistically, was the safest way to prevent my ass from being shot off.

After basic training in San Antonio, Texas, I was ready for cook's school. Or was I? One day I was summoned to a tent where two officers in combat fatigues and berets were waiting. They were members of the elite Air Commando Squadron and were recruiting individuals with 'street smarts and traits.' From there it was off to Fort Bragg, North Carolina, for combat training and then on to counter intelligence school at the US Army's School, Fort Holibard, Maryland. After six months of training I ended up at Edwards Air Force Base, California, any single man's dream. I worked counter intelligence in the Supply Division with several classified projects. One memorable incident occurred when the Air Police Security Patrols noticed a van parked in the surrounding mountains on certain days when test aircraft were being flown over the base. The commanding officer of the Office of Special Investigation pulled all of the agents in and we needed to identify, and put the individual, under surveillance. We set up a long distance surveillance in conjunction with a test flight of a classified aircraft. The interloper was at his location and we apprehended him. He was a Soviet consular official taking photographs and conducting intelligence operations. The matter was turned over to the Federal Bureau of Investigation.

Two weeks later I was on my way to Tuy Hua, Vietnam. This sand pit on the South China Sea was being developed as an air base to support our military operations in the country. Our role was diversified, from developing counterinsurgency plans and physical protections to assisting other US military and non-military special operations components with their tasking, in the field.

When I returned from Vietnam, I was assigned to the 1st Air Defense Command at Newburgh Air Base in New York. Seven months later I was honorably discharged. Back in Brooklyn, I wanted to become a police officer. I had applied and passed the New York City Police Department and Port Authority examinations. While waiting, I worked for a former FBI agent in his investigative firm in New York. I attended John Jay College of Criminal Justice at night and received an Associate Degree in Criminal Justice. The Port Authority hired me in January 1973 and I entered the Police Academy. That same day, the New York Police Department called me to enter their Academy. I turned them down. This was fortunate for me in that several of my Academy classmates who went over to the New York Police Department themselves were laid off when the economic disaster hit the city. I still had a good job.

My first assignment was at John F. Kennedy International Airport (JFKIA) with the screening program. We were assigned to the boarding gates during passenger screening, the result of international air piracy. It was a great job, inside, easy work, plenty of women to admire. I worked my way out of the Federal screening program and had various assignments including foot patrol at the international arrivals building. From time to time I was sent up to the Detective Division as a police officer for training, evaluation and to fill position deficiencies. When Menacham Begin, the Prime Minister of Israel, arrived at JFKIA, I was assigned to his security detail. I walked side-by-side with him down the tarmac to his waiting vehicle as my relatives in the Middle East were probably rolling over in their graves.

One morning after I had worked the 5x1 shift, the phone awakened me from a dead sleep. It was Captain Jack Boland, my commanding officer. 'Peter,' he said, 'I have some good news and some bad news, which one do you want first?' I said, 'Give me the bad news first and I can sleep on the good news.' He said, 'Well, I put you in for your detective's promotion today and it was turned down.' 'It figures,' I said to myself. 'Okay. What else Captain?' 'They promoted you to sergeant effective today. Congratulations, I am sorry to see you move on but it is a good career move.'

I regretted leaving the Police Unit at JFKIA, having established many good working relationships with my brothers and sisters in the department, and the general working population at the airport.

My arrival at the World Trade Center Command was exciting. The World Trade Center, the largest building complex in the world, was a city within a city. This was an engineering marvel surpassed by none. The complex not only represented the might of the Port Authority, but enhanced the Authority's posture as a viable corporate entity in a state where most government agencies were sub par to say the least.

My first assignment was strike duty. The local electrical workers union was on strike and we kept the peace. Once the strike was over, I received on the job training regarding the command and responsibilities of a tour commander. During the normal work day, the police commanding officer, staff lieutenant and staff sergeant augmented the sergeant on duty. In the afternoon and evening, the sergeant was the only police supervisor on duty at the complex with an enormous amount of responsibility. Most of the working population left after six in the evening and the complex was then in a partial shutdown mode except for the restaurants and cleaning personnel.

The Port Authority's push to sell floor space included informing potential tenants of the twenty-four hour presence of police officers in the building: a very positive variable in the marketing program. When a police officer or sergeant was assigned to the command he or she had to attend two weeks of high-rise firefighting training at the Mahwah, New Jersey fire training complex. We were the first responders to a fire alarm and were prepared to engage a fire until the arrival of the New York City Fire Department. We had our share of fires, small but still dangerous, and usually put them out before the arrival of the Fire Department.

The complex was safe for the most part. Crimes against the person were limited to the usual office disagreements and the occasional robbery on the concourse. The biggest crime problem was caused by what I like to call the 'typewriter and word processor fairy.' Every morning, police offices were dispatched to offices to prepare criminal complaints for theft of office equipment and other personal valuables. This was difficult to understand with the building in a partial operational mode and with security guards manning the open egress points, requiring identification for off hours entry. Approximately a year after I had been at the command, I was offered the staff sergeant position in the back office. This was an 8x4 day shift with weekends and holidays off. My wife was elated and I accepted the position.

My primary responsibilities were to update all of the emergency response procedures at the complex according to an established monthly program. The procedures would be reviewed and changes submitted to the commanding officer for his approval and then on to police headquarters. I also assisted

76

the staff lieutenant with all of the administrative paperwork. I supervised the crime prevention officer and assisted in the development of tenant related programs. Working at the Trade Center exposed me to the many facets of the Port Authority administrative and operational functions. The Port Authority, despite the usual union squabbles, was viewed as a family; every face had a name. This did not last long when changes were made and the governors of both New Jersey and New York started placing their cronies in top management positions, with the result that interpersonal relationships began to erode.

The problem with office equipment walking out of the building continued to increase. With only four police officers to cover the complex during the evening shifts, it was difficult to place the officers in a position to apprehend the individuals. The detective unit was overwhelmed with complaint follow-up reports and had limited surveillance time. The commanding officer at the complex had several meetings with staff to identify and bring some resolution to the problem. It was apparent the merchandise was being taken out through the sub-grade levels. The World Trade Center had several lower levels, including parking. Early in January 1981 I was detailed by the commanding officer to inspect access to the lower levels of the complex.

There are several staircases which begin at the concourse level and proceed to the B4 lower level. I conducted a walk through survey of the staircases in Buildings #1 and #2 from the concourse to the B4 parking levels.

What I determined was not surprising. One has to remember that when the complex was being built, like most large structures it did not include sophisticated state of the art security systems in the original plans. Although security was a concern, it was not paramount.

Inspection of the staircases leading to the subgrade parking level revealed a security nightmare. All the doors leading to the various parking levels were unlocked. There were alarm contact points in place but the system was not operational. The fire hoses were unraveled in some instances with the nozzles missing. There was evidence of marijuana use in the stairwells. It was apparent that entry into and egress from Buildings #1 and #2 through the staircases was accomplished unhampered by the existing security system. At certain points the doors to and from the parking lots were propped open by the fire nozzles. Obviously, this was one major contributing factor to the 'walking typewriter problem.' I remember making several recommendations to shore up the security lapses, including locking the doors, activating the intrusion alarms to police desk, and installing signing and video cameras in certain locations. I am not sure if this was ever accomplished in its entirety.

The World Trade Center was always in the public eye. We had an individual walk between the two towers on a tightrope. Then there was the psychotic who managed to elude all security systems and end up standing on the three foot wide ledge outside of one of the buildings on the 110th floor. He was professing his religious beliefs, using English and a language yet to be deciphered. If you want an empty feeling just look down from the top of the tower to the street without the security of windows. The building was built to sway, and it did. While we were talking to this messenger from who knows where, the New York Police Department Emergency Services Unit hooked up one of their officers to a safety harness. The subject was distracted, at which time the officer went over the side of the building and grabbed him.. He was brought to safety and sent on to Bellevue Psycho ward. Kudos to the officer from the New York Police Department's Emergency Services Unit who risked his life to save a disturbed person.

I remained at the World Trade Center for a time until I was promoted to detective sergeant and reassigned to my old command at JFKIA. I supervised the Detective Units at JFKIA and LaGuardia Airport with other detective sergeants. I continued to attend night school and received a Bachelor of Science degree in Criminal Justice from the New York Institute of Technology.

While at John F. Kennedy International Airport we had a terrible experience with a domestic terrorist group called the May 19th Communist Coalition. They were protesting against the arrival of the Springbok team from South Africa. A riot erupted and they threw mason jars filled with muriatic acid at the officers, seriously injuring one of my classmates. He unfortunately lost his eyesight in this terrible incident. We arrested the group only to have a local judge put them back on the streets with low bail.

When it came time to court hearings, all of the group's members appeared except one. An arrest warrant was issued and we spent years looking for this woman to no avail. The FBI joined in the fray and still we could not locate her. I continued to search for her in the bowels of Brooklyn, where I was raised. The Coalition had several locations and safe houses in Brooklyn and on my off duty time I would survey the locations and observe many members of the organization. However, the woman never materialized. She was never arrested and I often wonder if she died or perhaps was an informant working for the FBI. I often regret not being able to bring her to some form of justice for the damage she did to a dedicated officer's life over a political protest. Our constitution grants our citizens the right to protest, not to seriously injure police officers who are there to guarantee those rights are not interfered with.

I remained at JFKIA command until some time in late October 1982 when the superintendent of police recalled me to police headquarters. It was 1973 or 1974 when, as a rookie police officer, I had been detailed to assist the US Secret Service and a host of other law enforcement entities with the arrival of the Palestine Liberation Organization's Yasser Arafat and members of the PLO delegation. They were attending the United Nations General Assembly. I spent the next week literally in Yasser Arafat's face along with the US Secret Service. When Arafat departed he said goodbye and kissed on the cheeks the Secret Service agent assigned to protect him, and during this time our government embarrassed the country by having US Customs search the diplomatically protected luggage of the president of Lebanon, looking for explosives and weapons. The rockets flew on this one; nothing but apologies for the week by US officials. Did they actually think the president of Lebanon was smuggling weapons into the US?

My return to headquarters was a result of my writing memos for years citing a weak terrorist intelligence and response capability in our department. After meeting with facility commanding officers, who complained bitterly about their exposure to terrorist activity, the superintendent of police directed me to establish a program which was to assist commanding officers to develop their hostage and terrorist response plans, including the identification of critical targets.

This was an exciting time for me. I was back on the day shift. I was given an opportunity to provide some ideas and suggestions in the area of counter-terrorism. This subject had been a favorite of mine for many years and I had a penchant for reading and collecting any material on it. Only one problem developed with the program. I had no logistical support from within the organization to complete my task. I shared a secretary, and had to borrow a vehicle whenever I needed to travel amongst the various commands.

The commanding officers submitted their targeting studies for review but unfortunately they were not complete. They did not have the time or the expertise to properly dissect their commands, from a critical targeting aspect. I continued to assist with the studies and maintained an intelligence vigil with regard to Middle Eastern terrorist groups. For instance, the

Black June organization headed by Adu Nidal was allegedly sending 'hit' teams to the US, France and Italy. His purpose was to disrupt the convention of PLO terrorists who were scheduled to meet in the Middle East without his group being invited. The above-mentioned countries were members of the peacekeeping forces in Lebanon at the time. I made a recommendation to alert all commands regarding the potential of this type of activity by Abu Nidal. The response from command was to 'hold for additional information,' which I did.

A police department cannot operate an intelligence gathering unit without clear guidelines and a procedure outlining the handling of the material. I researched several police departments' intelligence gathering procedures, including the federal government's and, in 1983, promulgated, with the help of my commanding officer, the Terrorist/Planning/Intelligence guidelines procedure. This procedure outlined goals and objectives, and set the criteria for the collection, storage, and dissemination of police intelligence information. Also at this time, I was provided with a top secret security clearance by the Department of Justice. This clearance allowed me to receive classified information regarding potential problems posed by terrorists at our facilities.

One of the first programs I developed for the Department was the Crisis Management Organization Structure chart. This was done to establish an effective means of mitigating a crisis situation resulting from a terrorist attack. If I recall correctly, the policy formulation team consisted of the chairman of the Port Authority, executive director, assistant executive director, General Counsel, department directors, department heads and the superintendent of police. Pre-existing organizational authority had set the management role of the committee members. Within their scope of individual authority, their goal was to set and determine appropriate organizational policy responses to acts of terrorism within the jurisdiction of the Port

Authority. The second tier of the structure was the establishment of the Response Team. I believe the Comptroller, Public Relations, Law Department, Police Division and affected facility managers were members. The team was to be 'pro-active' in the organization's response to the crisis, utilizing pre-established strategies and resources. I cannot say with any certainty that this procedure was implemented; however, certain elements came into play in response to the World Trade Center bombing.

CHAPTER 7
Terrorist Targeting

During 1983 Middle East terrorists increased their activity within the region, expressing their position with the use of the car bomb. I had researched, and filed for police headquarters, several intelligence reports regarding the potential use of the car bomb within the United States. This prompted a memo to all commanding officers to be additionally vigilant in terminal frontage, government buildings, and limited parking areas. Our vulnerability to the international terrorist threat became clearer with the arrest of a Syrian national who had attempted to board a Royal Jordanian flight from Amsterdam to JFKIA with an estimated thirty pounds of explosives in his suitcases. The suitcases were outfitted with a timing device, preset to detonate after arrival at JFKIA.

We were no longer merely a spectator at the theater of international terrorism. We had become a targeted entity by virtue of our operation of international transportation facilities. Our immunity to terrorism was eroding. Additional concerns were being voiced by commanding officers at our facilities through various memoranda to the superintendent of police. They outlined their concerns regarding training, bomb threat response, upgraded weapons for police officers and some form of combat training to offset a frontal assault. During the beginning of 1984, I outlined the accomplishments of the Terrorist Planning and Intelligence Unit. I had compiled a manual describing terrorist groups and distributed it to commanding officers. Target and threat assessments were completed with the assistance of military units in the Port District, and our intelligence gathering capability had expanded greatly to include many interagency units. I also expressed my need for detectives to be assigned to the Unit. The collection and dissemination of real time intelligence was expanding and I needed help.

In January 1984 the level of Middle East terrorism did not decrease. I remember receiving a telephone call on a Saturday from the tour commander on duty at the World Trade Center. He had been advised of a threat made against the complex by a pro-Ayotollah Khomeini supporter. I contacted the Terrorist Task Force to receive further information. The individuals, two of them, were identified by an informant whose information had not been tested in the past. One individual was located and interviewed by the FBI, the other was wanted for questioning at that time. I relayed the information back to headquarters and also spoke with the commanding officer of the World Trade Center at his home, providing him with a complete update. The case was resolved without further incident.

This threat prompted the superintendent to direct me to the World Trade Center to develop a position paper on the vulnerability of the facility. Having worked at the World Trade Center Command, I had exclusive knowledge of some of the security weaknesses. I produced a three or four page assessment of the complex with the assistance of the Command. What I determined was disturbing from a security standpoint. Although the study was not all-inclusive, I do recall three areas of vulnerability that needed to be addressed.

The first was the subgrade area. The lower levels contained the 'nerve center' of the complex. There were cable vaults, telephone switching rooms, fuel bladders, reserve power generators, and a host of other systems that ran the complex. There were no intrusion systems in place. I judged the area to be a very vulnerable one, easily accessible and if it was attacked this would seriously affect the operation of the complex. I also addressed the problem of the truck dock entrance and perimeter of the complex. These too were highly vulnerable and easily penetrable. The security guards were not trained or prepared to handle any potential terrorist incursion into the complex. I specifically recall mentioning that the use of a car bomb in the subgrade could be a viable means by which the terrorists could accomplish their goals.

I believe I made several recommendations to address the immediate security lapses at the World Trade Center. One of the paramount problems was the fragmented security system in place. The police commanding officer should have had all the security functions under his command, including the training and supervision of security guards. Also needed was an increased police presence and security guards in the subgrade levels, perimeter and truck dock areas. I also made a suggestion that the superintendent of police should instigate a full vulnerability study at the complex to address potential terrorist attacks. Additional reports from the Crime Prevention Unit at the World Trade Center command were provided to the commanding officer outlining, I believe, essential operational components of the complex.

I remember meeting with some World Trade Center management people to discuss the vulnerabilities detailed in my report and recommendations. Their intention was to retain a consultant to perform the study of the complex.

I continued with my intelligence gathering and dissemination of the information. I had received several 'requests from Headquarters Command Staff' to review information in my files. I welcomed their increased interest. Their interest was not limited to just my files. They wanted access to the safe that contained classified information. I wrote the superintendent of police a memo detailing my responsibility as custodian of classified material and equipment. I was bound, as the custodian of the material, to conform to the federal guidelines covering disclosure. My position was clear. Nobody without a security clearance equal to the information requested would have access to the information. I also informed him that any further attempts at access would require me to alert the FBI. That put an end to the inquisitiveness of certain individuals. I continued developing my database on international terrorist groups.

With terrorism on the increase, and the increased vulnerability of the Port Authority to terrorism, Peter C. Goldmark, the executive director, created the Office of Special Planning in late 1984. In response, our union filed a host of grievances for violation of unit work clauses since I had been doing the work for years without logistical support. We maintained that detective sergeants had done the work and we owned that body of work under the memorandum of agreement. This dispute lasted for several years with one hearing after another. During this period, the Office of Special Planning conducted vulnerability studies of all the Port Authority facilities. Their reports were exceptional. They pointed outlines the vulnerabilities and recommended action to mitigate the weaknesses.

What I found most interesting about the creation of the Office of Special Planning was that their duties and responsibilities mirrored what I had been asked to accomplish years before. The unit had its own budget and several individuals with specialties conducive to forming a comprehensive unit. None of the members were of Middle Eastern background and none had any personal insight into the thinking processes of the Middle East. The makeup of the unit was a mixture of civilians and police officers, with only one officer of any rank – a captain. I knew the officers assigned and maintained a cordial and professional relationship with them.

Unfortunately, Peter Goldmark's establishment of the unit, no matter how well intended, fragmented the Port Authority's approach to countering potential terrorist attacks. I was not permitted to participate with the Office of Special Planning because of the union situation and direct orders from the superintendent of police. Here, the Port Authority had two units within the Police Unit doing similar jobs, neither of which communicated with the other. There was very little information exchanged or mutual utilization of expertise. Mixed signals were sent to both commanding officers and civilian management regarding the counter-terrorism program. Regardless, I continued with my intelligence gathering and my building a firm information exchange program.

When the Office of Special Planning completed studies of the various Port Authority facilities, they produced extensive reports on their findings. The reports were disseminated to various individuals. However, as the supervisor of the Terrorist Intelligence Unit, I was not on the distribution list. This was not a problem since control of these sensitive reports was tightly held, and the superintendent of police was on the list of recipients.

It was during this time period that I was called upon by many state and federal entities to assist them with their terrorist programs. The FBI placed me on their speakers bureau list and I traveled with their training section to various police academies. The FBI provided a presentation on domestic terrorist groups and I presented information on the Middle Eastern groups, their mindset and other related information. When the information about the program was picked up by other law enforcement and military entities, the requests for assistance became overwhelming. The superintendent of police was cooperative and allowed me to travel extensively, providing training and intelligence assistance when requested.

I honed my expertise, and our liaisons with other intelligence entities flourished. I assisted the FBI agent assigned to Interpol with the formulation of ALEAN (Airport Law Enforcement Agencies Network). I had found that the Category X airports in the United States were lagging in the intelligence and information sharing discipline. These police commands did not have active intelligence units dedicated to criminal and terrorist intelligence full-time. The nation's airports were the gateway for terrorists to enter our country. Most major airports experienced similar criminal problems. The common denominator we shared was that the law enforcement entities at our nation's airports had to wait for the FBI or some other federal law enforcement agency to provide information regarding traveling terrorists or associated activity.

With the help of the FBI's assigned agent, we created ALEAN. Interpol agreed to direct mail, call or fax international intelligence information directly to the Category X airports. This cooperative agreement filled an information void and expedited the messaging of critical intelligence information directly to the police. The establishment of ALEAN also allowed for the Category X airports to directly exchange information. I have to acknowledge that our superintendent of police was most supportive of the concept and allowed me the leeway to proceed and accomplish the goals of the organization. His support in this project was never wavering and his guidance on organizational problems was forthcoming.

We established a two-tier concept. The policymakers for the organization were the chiefs of police, or public safety directors, of the membership. The operational unit was made up of individuals such as myself who were responsible for the daily handling of communications and associated issues. The program was going very well, with information flowing smoothly amongst the airports. We would meet twice yearly at a different airport within the country and take care of business. ALEAN today boasts some eight members who have a commanding voice in Washington with the Federal Aviation Administration and congressional leaders.

Terrorism in the Middle East had not subsided. The Port Authority, after having the JFK International Airport vulnerability study completed, wanted to obtain a second opinion by hiring outside consultants. The Office of Special Planning had completed its study, and supposedly the unit was premier in the organization's counter-terrorist effort. Why then spend good taxpayer money on hiring an outside consultant who would only duplicate the Special Planning Unit's report after they read it? The Port Authority's management approach was to study the problem to death, refusing to resolve the real issues contained in the report. I advised the superintendent of police about conducting background investigations on the companies bidding before letting the contracts. He agreed and I subsequently contacted the director of aviation of the Port Authority and met with him to obtain basic information on the companies. The companies in this case were owned by and their principals were, former Israeli intelligence and military officers.

There were at least six Israeli companies that had bid on the contract. I initiated an investigation into the background of the principals and the companies. I utilized most of my intelligence and law enforcement sources to acquire the information. Prior to my completion of the investigation, someone in the Port Authority had hired one of the companies for US$75,000. The firm was to study JFKIA, LaGuardia and Newark airports. My investigation uncovered a mass of damaging information. Members of the firm were accused in Israel of murdering two Palestinian terrorists in custody and then attempting to cover up the criminal act. I alerted the superintendent of police who directed me to meet with the executive director of the Port Authority. At the meeting was the director of aviation, deputy director of aviation, and a member of the Port Authority's Law Department. Needless to say, there were some really upset executives after my briefing. The question was asked, 'who let the contract before Det. Sgt Caram finished his investigation?' The question was never answered and I gathered it was an inside political favor which totally embarrassed the organization.

The Port Authority was not immune from the attentions of the press. On April 9, 1987, James Peters and Don Singleton reported the whole story in the *New York Daily News*. The article quotes an unidentified spokeswoman as saying, 'We were no longer satisfied with the agreement.' I received several congratulatory notes from Police Command staff, the best including the observation, 'You sure called it.' I backgrounded other companies and a British firm won the contract. They were all former special air service members with distinguished records. I had the opportunity to have dinner with them one evening and enjoyed hearing their exploits recounted in their British accents. The group went on to complete their studies without my participation and I never got to see the final report. I was informed that their report was very complimentary to the report prepared by the Office of Special Planning. I expected this would happen. Years later when I assumed command of the Special Planning Unit, I found that their report was not in the files. Who had it? How damaging was the report?

The conflict between the Port Authority and the Sergeant's Union continued for several years. We continued to file unit work violations, improper practice charges, and sought a remedy for the Port Authority's intransigent position on the contract issue. This argument included hearings before an impartial arbiter from the American Arbitration Association in New York City. I attended over one hundred hearings and testified at least fifty times with regard to the issue. Everyone's patience and resolve began to wither under the extreme pressure and cost of the engagement. Finally, the Port Authority, on or about the same time a new contract was being negotiated, relented before the arbitrator. Just like that, the Office of Special Planning was abolished.

I assumed command of the new Special Planning Unit

sometime in July 1988. My job duties, however, became diluted, the result of a negotiated agreement. I, along with two other detective sergeants, became autonomous at Police Headquarters under the Criminal Investigation Bureau. We were to share each other's workload and in case of a deficiency in one of the positions we would cover the workload internally. This concept was agreed upon by the union. The other two sergeants who supervised the Internal Affairs Unit did not have a security clearance, and neither had any indepth knowledge of my unit's work or terrorist intelligence operations. I became the vacation relief sergeant, covering both the administrative sergeant's job and the Internal Affairs job when they were absent. I never knew where I would be each day. I would spend days doing overtime and vacation runs and charts and filing court notices for the detectives. I would be out in the field with the Internal Affairs Unit conducting investigations a week at a time. My workload never changed and I was under a lot of stress trying to keep up with world terrorist operations and doing detective roll calls – so much for the priority of public safety.

The Special Planning Unit consisted of myself, two untrained detectives, two or three civilian writers, security specialists, and a secretary. Our offices were located in a commercial building near Police Headquarters, segregated from the eyes of the world. I reviewed the existing vulnerability studies, the ones completed and the studies that had to be completed. In the interim, I sent my two detectives on a crime prevention course.

We continued with the studies and our intelligence gathering. With the potential for terrorist activity increasing as a result of the tensions with Iraq, the unit produced a lengthy threat assessment update. Keep in mind, daily reporting of intelligence was continuing and this report was issue specific regarding attack options Saddam Hussein could utilize through his surrogate terrorist allies. I believe this report was written in the late 1980s. The following January, in keeping with my reporting tradition, I filed a review of our accomplishments. The newest advantage was that I had been granted the use of a secure telephone system by the National Security Agency. The system allowed for the discussion of sensitive and/or classified material over the telephone. There were rigid controls associated with the use of the system and I, being the only person cleared, had exclusive use of it. I was also designated the department's custodian of records, and primary representative in this venue.

During the early part of 1991 I sent a status report to my commanding officer regarding the vulnerability studies. Our operation had run into a snag. My unit had been decimated with regard to personnel, from seven people to a total of three and an answering machine. The Port Authority was not concerned about the delays encountered with the follow up audits on the recommendations. The superintendent, however, was not happy at all. The line departments did not want to submit their responses to the recommendations in writing; rather, they wanted on-site discussions with the responses being hand scribed by my two detectives. This was a logistical and time management disaster given the depleted status of my unit. I continued to seek cooperation from the departments involved, to no avail. We encountered months of delays in the audit process.

Highlighting the importance of the overall security condition were the hostilities in the Middle East. During my vacation that summer, I received a visit from military intelligence at my home. The officers had contacted Police Headquarters requesting assistance and were directed to my residence. Their visit was not unusual; I often had visits on weekends from various intelligence entities. They requested my assistance prior to the initiation of the Desert Storm operation. I called the superintendent of police advising him of the request. He authorized my participation, on my own time. He advised me that he could not pay me overtime to assist the government. Okay, I spent three days of my own time, at a location, training certain special operations groups in the Islamic mindset and associated disciplines.

You really can't put a price on the men and women of our armed forces who are going into harm's way. This wasn't the first or last time I would volunteer my time in similar instances. I was a Vietnam veteran and appreciated the dedication of our armed forces. I returned from vacation to a host of intelligence reports and memos that had to be read and answered. During the year, I wrote intelligence updates on such groups as the Popular Front for the Liberation of Palestine General Command, Hamas–Islamic Resistance Movement, Hezbollah– Party of God in Iran, and the Popular Front. My intelligence reports and others' indicated increased activity against US targets in response to our peace initiative in the Middle East. Our problems with the line departments over the audit of the studies did not go away. We were at an impasse with regard to these. I decided to bring the problem into the open. On December 11, 1991, I wrote a three page position paper outlining the problems we had encountered. I also reminded the command staff of the executive director's mandate with regard to compliance with our requests. The superintendent of police had departed and been replaced by an auditor. I never received a reply to my memo. However, I was told to put the audits on hold until the problem could be resolved. This never happened. The audits for the most part stopped.

Intelligence analysts had begun to issue public cautions regarding the possibility that terrorist attacks could be forthcoming in response to the new peace initiative by the United States in the Middle East. There were several rejection-ist groups who wanted to scuttle the peace talks and had the capability to attack US targets. We also learned after the downing of the Pan American flight over Scotland that the device used had been manufactured in West Germany. There were also indications that Semtex, an explosive, was being masked with epoxy to avoid K-9 detection and that radio cassettes were being outfitted with bombs. This really increased the threat to aviation and all radios being brought on to airplanes were being turned on at screening points.

Terrorism, unlike conventional conflicts, does not have a well defined pattern of predictability. However, Islamic terrorism and the melding of violence and religion has some consistent elements enabling its interpretation. For instance, when there is a perception of political repression, social inequality and economic despair, the segment of society which is being manipulated seeks redress. Religion and clergy now become the interceder between man and his God and thus develop tangible control over the aggrieved parties. The frequency of physical acts of terrorism, the bombings, kidnappings and associated activity inevitably fluctuates. However, the volatile rhetoric will always continue, being our effective method of controlling the ideology of the easily influenced population.

While the Middle East was experiencing various degrees of violence, the rest of the modern world became a much more attractive target. Why were there no bombs in the Jewish communities of New York, no machine gun assaults, and no kidnappings between a very large ethnically diverse Jewish and Arabic community? There were plenty of opportunities to conduct operations and the hardware was readily available. The answer is rather easily definable. There was no economic or political repression. For instance, the Arab store owner on Atlantic Avenue probably had his merchandise delivered by an organization operated by Jewish businessmen. 'Money' rules the world, politics later, is the mindset of these emergent communities.

Don't get me wrong, there were problems. For example, we

all saw verbal engagements at times and low level personal assaults by individuals expressing their argumentative passion. However, the activity was pale compared with what was happening in the Middle East and the rest of the world. The lack of hard core terrorist activity in the United States and variable activity in the world lulled the Port Authority managers and police hierarchy into a lethargic posture, despite my constant intelligence reporting and analysis.

Among my warnings to the Port Authority, one event stands out. On February 26, 1992, a homemade device detonated on Second Avenue near a building housing the Syrian Mission to the United Nations. A communique stating 'Free Syrian Jews – more to follow' was recovered. I reported the incident, via memo, to my commanding officer and copied the memo to all command staff. The next day, the second highest police official at headquarters wrote a memo to the director of public safety, claiming that the threat level to the Port Authority was down due to the 'dissolution of the Soviet Union.' He further argued that intelligence was available through our detective unit at JFKIA and police commanders were dealing directly with other agencies when it came to obtaining intelligence information. He also suggested that the Special Planning Unit be dissolved and that my two detectives be reassigned to JFKIA Detective Unit to handle increases in cargo theft.

The official had not read the memo from the day before regarding the bombing in New York City. Nevertheless, we had a good working relationship with other agencies who provided information that was issue specific to a threat at a particular command. The information was what we like to call 'washed.' None of the commanders or the detectives had security clearances and the information was always forwarded to me for authentication and analysis. Not surprisingly, the Detectives Union and the Sergeants Union filed additional unit work violations against the police unit.

My unit was the only entity left in the Port Authority dedicated to terrorist intelligence and vulnerability studies and this individual wanted to utilize our expertise to investigate cargo crimes. Whatever happened to the protection of the traveling and working public at Port Authority facilities? Did the official bother to read the memos accumulating over the years regarding terrorist activities at transportation facilities worldwide?

While the internal battle continued, I was asked to provide a presentation in conjunction with the US State Department and FBI to over 300 law enforcement agents and officers in New York City. I had two hours to conduct my training and interestingly enough there were commanding officers from my department in the audience. Upon completion of the presentation, the agents were kind enough to take me to lunch and expressed their serious concern regarding the decision to farm my unit out. I had earned their support and I was gratified that they were going to be supportive of me at their next commanding officers meeting. I learned that they kept their word and raised 'holy terror' at the Port Authority's political decision to abandon the terrorist program. They understood the vulnerability of their commands to international terrorist activity.

Once again, I found myself embroiled with internal politics, trying to save the Special Planning Unit and Terrorist Intelligence Unit from becoming extinct. I was directed to meet with, and assist, the auditors from management and engineering with their politically motivated study of my unit. Remember, the interim director of public safety was the former director of the Audit Department, and the 'expert' assigned to review my unit worked for him while he was at the ivory tower. The reviewer had literally no idea what Islamic terrorism was or about the groups with a terrorist philosophy. His job was to disable my unit. I left him to his job and continued with my duties.

To that end, in March of the same year, I prepared a report called 'Militant Islam.' There had been increased activity in the Middle East by several prominent Islamic groups. Saudi Arabia, Algeria and Lebanon along with Israel were the recipients of the new Islamic initiative. I described, once again, the activities of the Party of God (Hezballah), Islamic Jihad and the Muslim Brotherhood. If you recall, the World Trade Center bombers were members of Hamas, which was spawned by the Muslim Brotherhood. The unification of these groups was once again rooted in protest against US Middle East policy.

The Special Planning Unit had been requested to study the truck dock at the World Trade Center and make security recommendations. Approximately the same time as the report was completed, the hatchet unit filed their politically motivated analysis and recommendations. This was about April 1992, if my memory serves me correctly. I am very clear with regard to their expressed findings. The report was exactly what I had expected. The contents were similar in tone and the recommendations echoed the earlier memo written by the senior police official.

The first recommendation was to disband the Special Planning Unit, claiming our current workload did not justify a separate unit. The best claim was 'world terrorism has subsided.' It should be pointed out that these individuals were not counter-terrorist specialists. There was a recommendation to suspend further activity on security hardening audits. They claimed all the audits were completed. This was nonsense. In 1991, my annual report indicated to the same police official that we were in the process of continuing with the audits. We had just scheduled the World Trade Center for the audit to ensure compliance with recommendations. They further argued that expertise and resources were no longer available. The report also had some lines such as 'long since reached diminishing returns on audit.' This was absurd: we had not completed the audits.

This report did highlight one thing: the true political position of the Port Authority towards counter-terrorism and public safety. Also clear from the report were two very important implications. The first was that the Port Authority officials no longer had any interest in pursuing the audits. The second was that they were no longer following up on the recommendations and that the efforts of public safety to pursue the recommendations of the audits were largely unanswered. This was a far cry from the original mandate in 1984 from then executive director Peter C. Goldmark. The report also admits we were in the process of conducting further studies at the World Trade Center.

This outrageous report undermined the counter-terrorist effort because it was distributed to senior police officials and management at the World Trade Center. The contents of the report fostered an unfounded belief that terrorism was no longer a threat to the organization, providing a political means for some individuals to pursue their egocentric agendas at the expense of public safety and security. I kept on working and our union kept on fighting the Port Authority.

I continued to issue my intelligence bulletins and quarterly assessments. Late in the year, I met with the commanding officer of the World Trade Center who wanted us to study the observation deck. The deck was a tourist attraction and maintained a high profile. I assigned my two detectives the task of doing the study while I managed the office and did other mandated administrative work at headquarters.

The New Year 1993 started with hot and heavy activity in the Middle East. The Islamic militants were once again swinging the sword. On January 22, 1993, I was doing an all-day presentation at Sing Sing Prison at the request of the New York State Commissioner of Corrects. The prison administrators were having difficulty handling prisoners of the Islamic faith and I provided guidance on the reduction of hostilities between the correction officers and the inmates. While on the way home, I was beeped by the commanding officer of the World Trade Center. I called him and he advised me that the detectives at JFKIA had received a call from the FBI with a terrorist threat warning directed at a high rise in New York. He needed more information and an analysis of the threat. (According to management and engineering, and a senior police official, terrorism was not an issue any longer.) I contacted the Terrorist Task Force, unfortunately, on an unsecure telephone. Two calls had been received in the Middle East with a demand, and if the demand was not met a high rise building in New York City would be bombed. No specific targets or groups making the threat were identified. I called the commanding officer of the World Trade Center and briefed him on what I had found out. I also recommended establishing a perimeter patrol around the World Trade Center. I did not receive any further updates regarding the threat. Just a little over a month later, the sword of Allah eviscerated the World Trade Center. Why didn't anyone listen?

CHAPTER 8
The Security Study

There is little doubt in anyone's mind that the Port Authority commissioned security and vulnerability studies to be completed at its facilities. There have been countless newspaper articles, governmental hearings, and civil depositions regarding the substance of these critical documents. The Port Authority's legal position is that these studies were considered 'self critical analysis,' and consequently should not be made available to the public or the plaintiffs' committee suing for damages. There is also concern that release of the report into the public domain would further deplete the security systems in place at the World Trade Center and would not be in the public interest.

The Port Authority is a quasi-public agency. They collect and expend millions of dollars of funds from the citizens of the region. We are the public interest! Clearly there has to be accountability by public officials to the constituency. The legal palaver and maneuvering is continuing as I write today. The Port Authority, to avoid further exposure of their failure in preventing the World Trade Center bombing, filed a motion in the Supreme Court of the State of New York on August 23, 2000, to quash my subpoena to testify and for a protective order preventing me from being deposed by attorneys for the individuals suing the Port Authority.

The Port Authority argued, 'Mr Caram was never assigned to the Office of Special Planning, established by Peter Goldmark and headed by Mr Edward O'Sullivan; his assignment as a Port Authority Detective Sergeant did not place him a policy making role with respect to any decisions relevant to this case, and based on Mr Caram's role and placement in the chain of command with the Police division, he is not an individual that the Port Authority intends to produce in connection with this matter and as such he is not an individual who is in a position to give testimony binding upon the Port Authority.' The lawyers for the Port Authority went on to argue, 'although Mr Caram, while assigned as a Detective Sergeant, did at various times, have access to and serve as a liaison with various outside agencies providing intelligence information to the Port Authority Police as well as access to certain documents that have been identified as the 'security documents', his responsibility was to report information and findings to individuals charged with the responsibility of making policy decisions concerning such information. Mr Caram's testimony can only be cumulative, redundant, improper and/or irrelevant. We fail to see why Mr Caram should be produced.'[18]

The Port Authority could not sustain their argument. I was not assigned to the Office of Special Planning, that is correct. Earlier, I explained the history of the Terrorist Intelligence Unit, Office of Special Planning and ultimately the Special Planning Unit. Additionally, intelligence officers do not make policy; they provide information to leaders who make decisions regarding the substance of the information provided and its potential impact on the organization and public. How could my testimony be redundant? I was the terrorist intelligence officer and supervisor of the Special Planning Unit. Fortunately, the Honorable Stanley L. Sklar, Justice of the Supreme Court of the State of New York, saw through this ruse and ordered my deposition to be taken under supervision of a special referee.

An interesting development occurred during the legal maneuvering. The Port Authority that claimed I had nothing to offer at a deposition filed a motion before the special referee claiming for the purpose of the deposition that I should be considered an employee of the Port Authority under their legal representation. Their argument was that I was not an independent witness and could not waive privileges or confidentiality. I informed the hearing officer that I rejected all legal representation and did not ask for Port Authority legal assistance. I was an independent person and business entity with no ties to any of the parties. Unfortunately, the special referee had ruled earlier on the motion, and the Port Authority prevailed in their ability to limit my testimony. Clearly, I felt and still do feel my First Amendment rights were infringed by a political machine run amuck. Depositions are held to explore and obtain knowledge, presumably the truth or knowledge a person may possess regarding a particular incident. The Port Authority's claim of right of privilege with regard to their former employees' testimony is manipulative of the public's interest, contrary to the mandate given the Port Authority, which was to serve as a public agency for the benefit of the public. My testimony lasted for two days and cumulatively was 250 pages long. In spite of the contention that I had nothing to offer of any substance, anyone reading the transcript will be able to garnish plenty of information not previously put on the record.

We as Americans are trusting and forgiving. It is in our nature. We take great pride in our system of government and blindly trust our elected and appointed officials to provide a sense of security in our everyday life. We rarely question what we don't see, partly because we are dedicated to conducting our own individual lives, and because of our underlying trust in the decision-making process of others. Unfortunately, the six people who died in the World Trade Center bombing, and the thousands injured, and the businesses disrupted were victimized by their blind trust of officials charged with providing a secure working environment.

The World Trade Center Security Study was developed to expose the complex's security weaknesses to terrorist attacks and to provide and enhance a secure working environment for the occupants of the building. I doubt if the occupants other than some Port Authority officials ever knew of the security problems in the complex or that a vulnerability study was being conducted.

The study was approximately 150 pages long. I recall it being very explicit in developing scenarios of attacks which could be conducted by terrorists against one of the most symbolic targets in the world. The report also provided recommendations to reduce the possibility of an attack or deflect terrorists away from the complex. There were a host of security deficiencies at points I had previously defined as critical targets, which if attacked would seriously affect the operation of the complex.

One of the most critical targets was public parking. I alluded to parking in the subgrade levels in my preliminary report of January 17, 1984, as being very vulnerable to a vehicle bomb. The OSP report on the World Trade Center further expanded this concept and recommended the elimination of public parking at the complex. How was this conclusion arrived at? One only had to look at world events during this time. There was a proliferation of car bombs as a method of expression by terrorists all over the world. Vehicle bombs were reportedly going off in Spain, Columbia, Lebanon, Sicily, and of course Northern Ireland. The frequency of car bombings increased so much that the world media rarely continued reporting them in depth. The World Trade Center was not protected from such an attack. Port Authority officials argued that closing the 400 space public parking area would have an economic impact on 'how we do business.' Additional arguments that 'the public would not stand for this capitulation to fear of terrorists' was only a lame excuse not to implement good security practices.

To the best of my knowledge, no one from Port Authority management consulted the tenants in the building with questions regarding the economic impact of eliminating public parking. The revenue to the Port Authority may have been impacted in a *de minimus* amount for the short term; however, the spaces could have easily been rented to tenants and their employees, at probably increased revenues.

Terrorists have many goals. One of their primary goals is to make a government alter its operations and to impact on how that government conducts business. We, as a free and democratic society, should use caution when enacting legislation impacting on the citizens of our great country in reaction to actual or potential terrorist activity. It is imperative that democratic governments adjust to changing political times with respect to protecting their citizens. Our political system inherently provides the citizenry with the ability to monitor, contribute and negate changes to our constitutionally earned freedom. The real impact here would have been perhaps a *de minimis* short-term loss of revenue to the Port Authority.

Further evidence of the 'spin' utilized by the Port Authority in an attempt to explain away the flawed security concept is evidenced at the airports operated by the Authority. When skyjacking of international and domestic flights became a terrorist method, the United States, through the Federal Aviation Administration, enacted strict airport security guidelines in cooperation with the international aviation community. These measures were the screening of passengers and stationing of police officers at the screening points. Were there constitutional concerns regarding intrusion and warrantless searches? Of course there were! Was there oversight to insure our constitutionally earned freedoms were not trampled upon? Is airline travel much safer now as a result of the Auti-Terrorist Skyjacking Program? Are the airlines going out of business or suffering financial losses due to this security innovation? Is the Port Authority still making money as the airport operator? Is the American public inconvenienced to some degree? Yes, however, we adjusted with little fanfare.

Eventually, Port Authority Police officers were removed from individual air line gates and corridors for screening established. Once again safety was traded off for cost effectiveness. A five minute response plan was put into effect, diminishing the effectiveness of the screening points and eventually the entire air travel network in the United states.

Inconvenience should not be used to bar good security practices. To argue economic impact and constitutional infringement in lieu of security adjustments to an obvious potential security condition is just a 'spin' to avoid accountability.

I have testified at hearings and depositions that to immediately shut down all parking at the complex was a knee jerk reaction. The vital area of the subgrade levels that house the parking garages and integral operating systems was the focus of many security recommendations in the security study. The implementation of these recommendations in tandem with the elimination of public parking, I believe, would have hardened this particular critical target area and greatly deterred the World Trade Center bombing. The fact is that the terrorist drove into an unsecured public parking lot, unchallenged and undetected. The area was chosen because the terrorist did a site security evaluation and determined the area selected was 'soft and unprotected.' Investigation revealed that bombing suspect Ibrahim Elgabrowny attended two seminars in construction at the World Trade Center during 1992 – the latest being on December 1, 1992 – just prior to the bombing. There was little risk of discovery, and exfiltration could be accomplished without challenge.

The Port Authority conducted a search for an outside security consultant to conduct a vulnerability study of the World Trade Center. This was accomplished some time, I believe, in mid-1986. Why restudy the World Trade Center? I suspect the OSP report was so critical and to the point that the officials at the Port Authority wanted another opinion. Why challenge one's own expert findings? More important, why expend additional taxpayer dollars to the tune of approximately US$100,000? Did anyone at the Port Authority really think the findings of the consultant would be any different from those of their own in-house experts?

Although I did not participate in either the OSP or Science Applications International Corporation studies, both of these highly professional reports found similar security deficiencies at the World Trade Center, paying special attention to the subgrade areas and public parking. These reports determined that access to the subgrade level using vehicles was blatantly uncontrolled. The joint recommendation to install vehicle barriers and eliminate public parking were unmistakably clear and pronounced.

The newspaper headlines read 'Detonation Disabled Evacuation Plan Center.'[19] The article states how the blast rendered the operating systems useless. Stanley Brezenoff, Port Authority Executive Director, was quoted as saying, 'The major problem we faced was we could not communicate with the people stranded on the upper floors or stairwells, and there was no light.'[20] Charles Makish, the director of the World Trade Center, is quoted in the same article as saying, 'I don't think anybody anticipated the magnitude of this blast. It was absolutely enormous.'[21] The article reports how the explosion 'destroyed the primary and emergency power systems and knocked out telephones, the public address system and closed-circuit television system.'[22] There is little doubt the emergency evacuation plans and communications capabilities were rendered useless by the blast. The recommendations to relocate the emergency command center (Police Desk and fire communications system) and establish a satellite communications system independent of the host system were included in both of the studies. They were not implemented.

The vulnerability studies did 'anticipate' the impact of a terrorist attack at the complex, especially the resultant damage from a car bomb.

The accepted practice that management can delegate authority but not responsibility is a staple in the philosophy of corporate security operations. On reflection, however, I believe that when public safety is at risk, the professionals in law enforcement are better suited to make these types of critical decisions. The management officials at the Port Authority are highly respected and innovative in their respective vocations. They are engineers and building operators. What they are not is counter-terrorist and security specialists. Earlier, I alluded to a fragmented security system. The review of the recommendations from the OSP and SAIC studies was done for the most part in cooperation with the Port Authority Police. The final decisions on the recommendations were left to individuals who as corporate executives only see the bottom line costs. This is the staple in the galaxy of corporate operations.

Port Authority officials were provided with attack scenarios, security recommendations, and intelligence reports over a period of time. They did not have the professional capacity to understand the impact of their decisions because their focus was corporate operations and not the realm of public safety. They arrogantly ignored the recommendations of even their own hired experts. The failure to allow the security professionals in the Port Authority's organization to apply their expertise to protect the public greatly enhanced the exposure and risk of the public to the terrorist bomb.

A functional security system is not talismanic. There should be clearly defined goals and an operational structure. A clear delineation of responsibility for the application of the principles and recommendations contained in the security plan should be visible and an integral part of the security system. The individuals making the decision to implement or not to implement recommendations should be well versed in the art of building security systems and independent of political interference. Their focus should be the task of providing security.

Unfortunately, the system in place at the time of the World Trade Center bombing was neither centralized nor cohesive. The intentions of the officials making the decisions were probably without malice. I do not doubt that. However, the question remains, what were their security qualifications? The decision makers were apprised of, even deluged with state of the art recommendations from their in-house experts and consultants. Why disregard the most critical area, the subgrade? One can reason that the decision makers felt their security prowess was greater than that of the experts or they felt that terrorists would not strike at the heart of the World Trade Center with a car bomb and adopted a philosophy of 'let's take a gamble, it won't happen.' Whatever the reason, the Port Authority's dysfunctional security system at the time further contributed to the overall meltdown of security at the complex.

The Port Authority realized its vulnerability to terrorist attacks. Security studies commenced approximately ten years prior to the bombing. The Authority developed its own in-house expertise, and then retained consultants. Recommendations as to critical targets and the reduction of the attractiveness of the targets were submitted for review. Decisions were then made by unqualified managers participating in the capacity of a security consortium. The potential *de minimis* loss of revenue appears to be the primary reason for the decision not to eliminate public parking. The Port Authority had the financial ability to implement the majority of recommendations. There was no clear delineation with regard to decision making and responsibility in regard to the vulnerability studies and overall security at the complex.

CHAPTER 9
The Port Authority's Dysfunctionality

In the preceding pages, I have endeavored to bring to light the many variables associated with the World Trade Center bombing. We live in a world that has changed dramatically, with a far-reaching impact on our perception of security. Our 'immunity from terrorism' is no longer a true claim. Our government's engagement in world affairs creates a pyramid of problems which must be recognized and addressed by our elected and appointed officials. My criticisms and exposure of the Port Authority's dysfunctional security system in place at the time of the World Trade Center bombing and the failure of our domestic and foreign intelligence operations hopefully will enable the victims and their families to understand better the variables which led to this tragic event. The policymakers at the Port Authority must determine the security priorities and key objectives, remembering that a secure working environment is paramount.

We, as humans, are not infallible. We are, by our given nature, forgiving and tolerant. Our expectations with regard to our military, law enforcement, and intelligence agencies performances are high. We expect, without reservation, that the officials charged with security should be competent and able to meet the challenges of countering terrorism. These are reasonable expectations.

Within this dimension of trust is also accountability. Leadership without accountability decreases the positive impact and undermines the inherent trust of the position. It would be novel to have an executive claim he accepts the responsibility for the security failures contributing to the World Trade Center bombing. Apparently, only redress through the courts will provide, at great cost, the insight and relief rightfully deserved by the victims who were physically and emotionally damaged by the World Trade Center bombing.

Today, as I conclude this book, it is the anniversary of the bombing, a time of personal reflection regarding the tragedy. I am amazed at the lessons we did not learn. Security in most buildings and airports has waned, our attitude once again complacent. Our vulnerability to attack is still very high. The only saving grace is that we are fortunate that the FBI and CIA have had many successful interceptions of potential terrorist attacks. We rarely hear of the success of these agencies and only dwell on their failures. However, the Jihad mentally is for eternity, not just a few years. The threat of nuclear or biological agents being used against the United States by Holy Warriors such as Bin Laden is significant and a real concern. The potential for cyber terrorism and attacks against our infrastructure remains constant and very real.

To emphasize the reality of the threat to our great country, the US Commission on National Security in the 21st Century published its findings in February 2001. The report is 130 pages in length and was formulated during the past few years. The commission is co-chaired by former US Senators Gary Hart and Warren B. Rudman.

The World Trade Center bombing of 1993 was only the first shot in the globalization of Islamic terror. The commission's report and findings clearly define our vulnerabilities and make sweeping recommendations to counter the ever present threat of terrorism to our country and society.

Finally, if we are to neutralize our adversary, we should take a lesson from our own history. The following extract is from 'The American Revolution: First Phase':

Bunker Hill was a Pyrrhic victory, its strategic effect

practically nil since the two armies remained in virtually the same position that they had held before. Its consequences, nevertheless, cannot be ignored. A force of farmers and townsmen, fresh from their fields and shops, with hardly a semblance of orthodox military organization, had met and fought on equal terms with a professional British Army. On the British this astonishing feat had a sobering effect, for it taught them that American resistance was not to be easily overcome; never again would British commanders lightly attempt such an assault on Americans in fortified positions. On the Americans, the effect was hardly sobering, and in the long run was perhaps not salutary. Bunker Hill, along with Lexington and Concord, went far to create the American tradition that the citizen soldier when aroused is more than a match for the trained professional, a tradition that was to be reflected in American military policy for generations afterward.[23]

End Notes

[1] You're probably wondering what we found out. Well, Sammy the Bull Gravano had Louie Dubono shot in the World Trade Center garage for showing disrespect to the Godfather John Gotti. It didn't end there. Our investigation uncovered widespread alleged involvement by the Gambino crime family.

[2] *The Arab Mind*, revised 1983, New York and The Arab Americans by Alixa Naff, 1988, Charles Scribner's Sons, New York, Philadelphia, Chelsea House Publishers.

[3] Abdullah, Yussif Ali, *The Holy Quran*, Brentwood, Maryland, Ammana Corp.

[4] Kolocotronis, Jamilah *Islamic Jihad: An Historical Perspective*. Indianapolis, Indiana, American Trust Publications.

[5] Ayatololah Ruhollah Khomeini in Kashf al-Asrar (*Key to the Secrets*), 1986. (Originally published in Qom in 1942 and reprinted in Tehran in 1980 and 1983.)

[6] These figures are based on various US Government reported numbers.

[7] The full text of this will by Rada Muhammad N'eman was published in Lebanon by Payam Shahid (Message of the Martyr) in a special issue, October 1985.

[8] Meaning Ayatollah Khomeini, who assumed the title of Imam.

[9] The desert of Karbala in southern Iraq is where Hussein, the third Imam of duodecimal Shi'ism, was killed in battle against the troops of the Umayid Caliph Yazid ben Muawyyah in the seventh century.

[10] Presumably the name of the writer's son.

[11] Sun Tzn, *The Art of War*, 500 BC.

[12] Information provided by FBI.

[13] 'The New Islamist International: Strike Force on Terrorism & Unconventional Warfare, February 1, 1993, US Congress.

[14] Intelligence Sources, US Government.

[15] *Newsweek* March 15, 1993.

[16] Ibid.

[17] *Jersey Journal*, Thursday, March 11, 1993.

[18] Gerald Crowley, Assistant Chief New York Litigation Division, Port Authority, Law Department, August 17, 2000.

[19] *Sunday Star-Ledger*, February 28, 1993.

[20] Ibid.

[21] Ibid.

[22] Ibid.

[23] 'The American Revolution: first phase', extracted from *American Military History*, Army Historical Series.

APPENDIX

The Charter of the Hamas
THE CHARTER OF ALLAH: THE PLATFORM OF THE ISLAMIC RESISTANCE MOVEMENT (HAMAS)

In the Name of Allah, the Merciful, the Compassionate.

You are the best community that has been raised up for mankind. Ye enjoin right conduct and forbid indecency; and ye believe in Allah. And if the People of the Scripture had believed, it had been better for them. Some of them are believers; but most of them are evil-doers.

They will not harm you save a trifling hurt, and if they fight against you they will turn and flee. And afterward they will not be helped.

'Ignominy shall be their portion wheresoever they are found save [where they grasp] a rope from Allah and a rope from man. They have incurred anger from their Lord, and wretchedness is laid upon them. That is because they used to disbelieve the revelations of Allah, and slew the Prophets wrongfully. That is because they were rebellious and used to transgress.' Surat Al-Imran (III), verses 109-111.

Israel will rise and will remain erect until Islam eliminates it as it had eliminated its predecessors.

The Islamic World is burning. It is incumbent upon each one of us to pour some water, little as it may be, with a view of extinguishing as much of the fire as he can, without awaiting action by the others.

INTRODUCTION

Grace to Allah, whose help we seek, whose forgiveness we beseech, whose guidance we implore and on whom we rely. We pray and bid peace upon the Messenger of Allah, his family, his companions, his followers and those who spread his message and followed his tradition; they will last as long as there exist Heaven and Earth.

O, people! In the midst of misadventure, from the depth of suffering, from the believing hearts and purified arms; aware of our duty and in response to the decree of Allah, we direct our call, we rally together and join each other. We educate in the path of Allah and we make our firm determination prevail so as to take its proper role in life, to overcome all difficulties and to cross all hurdles. Hence our permanent state of preparedness and our readiness to sacrifice our souls and dearest [possessions] in the path of Allah.

Thus, our nucleus has formed which chartered its way in the tempestuous ocean of creeds and hopes, desires and wishes, dangers and difficulties, setbacks and challenges, both internal and external.

When the thought matured, the seed grew and the plant took root in the land of reality, detached from temporary emotion and unwelcome haste, the Islamic Resistance Movement erupted in order to play its role in the path of its Lord. In so doing, it joined its hands with those of all Jihad fighters for the purpose of liberating Palestine. The souls of its Jihad fighters will encounter those of all Jihad fighters who have sacrificed their lives in the land of Palestine since it was conquered by the Companion of the Prophet, be Allah's prayer and peace upon him, and until this very day. This is the Charter of the Islamic Resistance (Hamas) which will reveal its face, unveil its identity, state its position, clarify its purpose, discuss its hopes, call for support to its cause and reinforcement, and for joining its ranks. For our struggle against the Jews is extremely wide-ranging and grave, so much so that it will need all the loyal efforts we can wield, to be followed by further steps and reinforced by successive battalions from the multifarious Arab and Islamic world, until the enemies are defeated and Allah's victory prevails. Thus we shall perceive them approaching in the horizon, and this will be known before long: 'Allah has decreed: Lo! I very shall conquer, I and my messenger, lo! Allah is strong, almighty.'

PART I - KNOWING THE MOVEMENT

The Ideological Aspects
Article One
The Islamic Resistance Movement draws its guidelines from Islam; derives from it its thinking, interpretations and views about existence, life and humanity; refers back to it for its conduct; and is inspired by it in whatever step it takes.

The Link between Hamas and the Association of Muslim Brothers
Article Two
The Islamic Resistance Movement is one of the wings of the Muslim Brothers in Palestine. The Muslim Brotherhood Movement is a world organization, the largest Islamic Movement in the modern era. It is characterized by a profound understanding, by precise notions and by a complete comprehensiveness of all concepts of Islam in all domains of life: views and beliefs, politics and economics, education and society, jurisprudence and rule, indoctrination and teaching, the arts and publications, the hidden and the evident, and all the other domains of life.

Appendix

Structure and Essence
Article Three
The basic structure of the Islamic Resistance Movement consists of Muslims who are devoted to Allah and worship Him verily [as it is written]: 'I have created Man and Devil for the purpose of their worship' [of Allah]. Those Muslims are cognizant of their duty towards themselves, their families and country and they have been relying on Allah for all that. They have raised the banner of Jihad in the face of the oppressors in order to extricate the country and the people from the [oppressors'] desecration, filth and evil.

Article Four
The Movement welcomes all Muslims who share its beliefs and thinking, commit themselves to its course of action, keep its secrets and aspire to join its ranks in order to carry out their duty. Allah will reward them.

Dimensions of Time and Space of the Hamas
Article Five
As the Movement adopts Islam as its way of life, its time dimension extends back as far as the birth of the Islamic Message and of the Righteous Ancestor. Its ultimate goal is Islam, the Prophet its model, the Quran its Constitution. Its special dimension extends wherever on earth there are Muslims, who adopt Islam as their way of life; thus, it penetrates to the deepest reaches of the land and to the highest spheres of Heavens.

Peculiarity and Independence
Article Six
The Islamic Resistance Movement is a distinct Palestinian Movement which owes its loyalty to Allah, derives from Islam its way of life and strives to raise the banner of Allah over every

inch of Palestine. Only under the shadow of Islam could the members of all regions coexist in safety and security for their lives, properties and rights. In the absence of Islam, conflict arises, oppression reigns, corruption is rampant and struggles and wars prevail. Allah had inspired the Muslim poet, Muhammad Iqbal, when he said:

'When the Faith wanes, there is no security
There is no this-worldliness for those who have no faith
Those who wish to live their life without religion
Have made annihilation the equivalent of life.'

The Universality of Hamas
Article Seven

By virtue of the distribution of Muslims, who pursue the cause of the Hamas, all over the globe, and strive for its victory, for the reinforcement of its positions and for the encouragement of its Jihad, the Movement is a universal one. It is apt to be that due to the clarity of its thinking, the nobility of its purpose and the loftiness of its objectives.

It is in this light that the Movement has to be regarded, evaluated and acknowledged. Whoever denigrates its worth, or avoids supporting it, or is so blind as to dismiss its role, is challenging Fate itself. Whoever closes his eyes from seeing the facts, whether intentionally or not, will wake up to find himself overtaken by events, and will find no excuses to justify his position. Priority is reserved to the early comers.

Oppressing those who are closest to you, is more of an agony to the soul than the impact of an Indian sword.

'And unto thee have we revealed the Scripture with the truth, confirming whatever scripture was before it, and a watcher over it. So judge between them by that which Allah hath revealed, and follow not their desires away from the truth which has come unto thee. For each we have appointed a divine law and a traced-out way. Had Allah willed, He could have made you

118

one community. But that He may try you by that which he has given you [He has made you as you are]. So vie with one another in good works. Unto Allah, you will all return. He will then inform you of that wherein you differ.'

Hamas is one of the links in the Chain of Jihad in the confrontation with the Zionist invasion. It links up with the setting out of the Martyr Izz a-din Ai-Qassam and his brothers in the Muslim Brotherhood who fought the Holy War in 1936; it further relates to another link of the Palestinian Jihad and the Jihad and efforts of the Muslim Brothers during the 1948 War, and to the Jihad operations of the Muslim Brothers in 1968 and thereafter.

But even if the links have become distant from each other, and even if the obstacles erected by those who revolve in the Zionist orbit, aiming at obstructing the road before the Jihad fighters, have rendered the pursuance of Jihad impossible; nevertheless, the Hamas has been looking forward to implement Allah's promise whatever time it might take. The prophet, prayer and peace be upon him, said: 'The time will not come until Muslims will fight the Jews (and kill them); until the Jews hide behind rocks and trees, which will cry: O Muslim! there is a Jew hiding behind me, come on and kill him! This will not apply to the Gharqad, which is a Jewish tree' (cited by Bukhari and Muslim).

The Slogan of the Hamas
Article Eight
Allah is its goal, the Prophet its model, the Qur'an its Constitution, Jihad its path and death for the case of Allah its most sublime belief.

PART II – OBJECTIVES

Motives and Objectives
Article Nine

Hamas finds itself at a period of time when Islam has waned away from the reality of life. For this reason, the checks and balances have been upset, concepts have become confused, and Values have been transformed; evil has prevailed, oppression and obscurity have reigned; cowards have turned tigers, homelands have been usurped, people have been uprooted and are wandering all over the globe. The state of truth has disappeared and was replaced by the state of evil. Nothing has remained in its right place, for when Islam is removed from the scene, everything changes. These are the motives.

As to the objectives: discarding the evil, crushing it and defeating it, so that truth may prevail, homelands revert [to their owners], calls for prayer be heard from their mosques, announcing the reinstitution of the Muslim state. Thus, people and things will revert to their true place.

Article Ten

The Islamic Resistance Movement, while breaking its own path, will do its utmost to constitute at the same time a support to the weak, a defense to all the oppressed. It will spare no effort to implement the truth and abolish evil, in speech and in fact, both here and in any other location where it can reach out and exert influence.

PART III – STRATEGIES AND METHODS

The Strategy of Hamas: Palestine is an Islamic Waqf
Article Eleven

The Islamic Resistance Movement believes that the land of

Palestine has been an Islamic Waqf throughout the generations and until the Day of Resurrection, no one can renounce it or part of it, or abandon it or part of it. No Arab country nor the aggregate of all Arab countries, and no Arab King or President nor all of them in the aggregate, have that right, nor has that fight any organization or the aggregate of all organizations, be they Palestinian or Arab, because Palestine is an Islamic Waqf throughout all generations and to the Day of Resurrection. Who can presume to speak for all Islamic Generations to the Day of Resurrection? This is the status [of the land] in Islamic Shari'a, and it is similar to all lands conquered by Islam by force, and made thereby Waqf lands upon their conquest, for all generations of Muslims until the Day of Resurrection. This [norm] has prevailed since the commanders of the Muslim armies completed the conquest of Syria and Iraq, and they asked the Caliph of Muslims, 'Umar Ibn al-Khaftab, for his view of the conquered land, whether it should be partitioned between the troops or left in the possession of its population, or otherwise. Following discussions and consultations between the Caliph of Islam, 'Umar Ibn ai-Khaftab, and the Companions of the Messenger of Allah, be peace and prayer upon him, they decided that the land should remain in the hands of its owners to benefit from it and from its wealth; but the control of the land and the land itself ought to be endowed as a Waqf [in perpetuity] for all generations of Muslims until the Day of Resurrection. The ownership of the land by its owners is only one of usufruct, and this Waqf will endure as long as Heaven and earth last. Any demarche in violation of this law of Islam, with regard to Palestine, is baseless and reflects on its perpetrators.

Hamas in Palestine: Its Views on Homeland and Nationalism
Article Twelve
Hamas regards Nationalism (Wataniyya) as part and parcel of

the religious faith. Nothing is loftier or deeper in Nationalism than waging Jihad against the enemy and confronting him when he sets foot on the land of the Muslims. And this becomes an individual duty binding on every Muslim man and woman; a woman must go out and fight the enemy even without her husband's authorization, and a slave without his masters' permission.

This [principle] does not exist under any other regime, and it is a truth not to be questioned. While other nationalisms consist of material, human and territorial considerations, the nationality of Hamas also carries, in addition to all those, the all important divine factors which lend to it its spirit and life; so much so that it connects with the origin of the spirit and the source of life and raises in the skies of the Homeland the Banner of the Lord, thus inexorably connecting earth with Heaven.

When Moses came and threw his baton, sorcery and sorcerers became futile.

Peaceful Solutions, [Peace] Initiatives and International Conferences
Article Thirteen

[Peace] initiatives, the so-willed peaceful solutions, and the international conferences to resolve the Palestinian problem, are all contrary to the beliefs of the Islamic Resistance Movement. For renouncing any part of Palestine means renouncing part of the religion; the nationalism of the Islamic Resistance Movement is part of its faith, the movement educates its members to adhere to its principles and to raise the banner of Allah over their homeland as they fight their Jihad: 'Allah is the all-powerful, but most people are not aware.'

From time to time a clamoring is voiced, to hold an International Conference in search for a solution to the problem. Some accept the idea, others reject it, for one reason or another, demanding the implementation of this or that condition, as a prerequisite for agreeing to convene the Conference or for participating in it. But the Islamic Resistance Movement, which is aware of the [prospective] parties to this conference, and of their past and present positions towards the problems of the Muslims, does not believe that those conferences are capable of responding to demands, or of restoring rights or doing justice to the oppressed. Those conferences are no more than a means to appoint the nonbelievers as arbitrators in the lands of Islam. Since when did the Unbelievers do justice to the Believers?

'And the Jews will not be pleased with thee, nor will the Christians, till thou follow their creed. 'Say: Lo! the guidance of Allah [himself] is the Guidance. And if you should follow their desires after the knowledge which has come unto thee, then you would have from Allah no protecting friend nor helper.' Sura 2 (the Cow), verse 120

There is no solution to the Palestinian problem except by Jihad. The initiatives, proposals and International Conferences are but a waste of time, an exercise in futility. The Palestinian people are too noble to have their future, their right and their destiny submitted to a vain game. As the hadith has it:

'The people of Syria are Allah's whip on this land; He takes revenge by their intermediary from whoever he wished among his worshipers. The Hypocrites among them are forbidden from vanquishing the true believers, and they will die in anxiety and sorrow.' (Told by Tabarani, who is traceable in ascending order of traditionades to Muhammad, and by Ahmed whose chain of transmission is incomplete. But it is bound to be a true hadith, for both story tellers are reliable. Allah knows best.)

The Three Circles
Article Fourteen
The problem of the liberation of Palestine relates to three

circles: the Palestinian, the Arab and the Islamic. Each one of these circles has a role to play in the struggle against Zionism and it has duties to fulfill. It would be an enormous mistake and an abysmal act of ignorance to disregard anyone of these circles. For Palestine is an Islamic land where the First Qibla and the third holiest site are located. That is also the place whence the Prophet, be Allah's prayer and peace upon him, ascended to heavens.

'Glorified be He who carried His servant by night from the Inviolable Place of worship to the Far Distant Place of Worship, the neighborhood whereof we have blessed, that we might show him of our tokens! Lo! He, only He, is the Hearer, the Seer.' Sura XVII (Al-Isra'), verse 1

In consequence of this state of affairs, the liberation of that land is an individual duty binding on all Muslims everywhere. This is the base on which all Muslims have to regard the problem; this has to be understood by all Muslims. When the problem is dealt with on this basis, where the full potential of the three circles is mobilized, then the current circumstances will change and the day of liberation will come closer.

'You are more awful as a fear in their bosoms than Allah. That is because they are a folk who understand not.' Sura LIX, (Al-Hashr, the Exile), verse 13

The Jihad for the Liberation of Palestine is an Individual Obligation
Article Fifteen
When our enemies usurp some Islamic lands, Jihad becomes a duty binding on all Muslims. In order to face the usurpation of Palestine by the Jews, we have no escape from raising the banner of Jihad. This would require the propagation of Islamic consciousness among the masses on all local, Arab and Islamic levels. We must spread the spirit of Jihad among the [Islamic] Umma, clash with the enemies and join the ranks of the Jihad

124

fighters.

The 'ulama as well as educators and teachers, publicity and media men as well as the masses of the educated, and especially the youth and the elders of the Islamic Movements, must participate in this raising of consciousness. There is no escape from introducing fundamental changes in educational curricula in order to cleanse them from all vestiges of the ideological invasion which has been brought about by orientalists and missionaries. That invasion had begun overtaking this area following the defeat of the Crusader armies by Salah a-Din el Ayyubi. The Crusaders had understood that they had no way to vanquish the Muslims unless they prepared the grounds for that with an ideological invasion which would confuse the thinking of Muslims, revile their heritage, discredit their ideals, to be followed by a military invasion. That was to be in preparation for the Imperialist invasion, as in fact [General] Allenby acknowledged it upon his entry to Jerusalem: 'Now, the Crusades are over.' General Gouraud stood on the tomb of Salah a-Din and declared: 'We have returned, O Salah-a-Din!' Imperialism has been instrumental in boosting the ideological invasion and deepening its roots, and it is still pursuing this goal. All this had paved the way to the loss of Palestine. We must imprint on the minds of generations of Muslims that the Palestinian problem is a religious one, to be dealt with on this premise. It includes Islamic holy sites such as the Aqsa Mosque, which is inexorably linked to the Holy Mosque as long as the Heaven and earth will exist, to the journey of the Messenger of Allah, be Allah's peace and blessing upon him, to it, and to his ascension from it.

'Dwelling one day in the Path of Allah is better than the entire world and everything that exists in it. The place of the whip of one among you in Paradise is better than the entire world and everything that exists in it. [God's] worshipers going and coming in the Path of Allah is better than the entire world and everything that exists in it.' (Told by Bukhari, Muslim Tirmidhi and Ibn Maja.)

I swear by that who holds in His Hands the Soul of Muhammad! I indeed wish to go to war for the sake of Allah! I will assault and kill, assault and kill, assault and kill (told by Bukhari and Muslim).

Article Sixteen

We must accord the Islamic [young] generations in our area, an Islamic education based on the implementation of religious precepts, on the conscientious study of the Book of Allah; on the Study of the Prophetic Tradition, on the study of Islamic history and heritage from its reliable sources, under the guidance of experts and scientists, and on singling out the paths which constitute for the Muslims sound concepts of thinking and faith. It is also necessary to study conscientiously the enemy and its material and human potential; to detect its weak and strong spots, and to recognize the powers that support it and stand by it. At the same time, we must be aware of current events, follow the news and study the analyses and commentaries on it, together with drawing plans for the present and the future and examining every phenomenon, so that every Muslim, fighting Jihad, could live out his era aware of his objective, his goals, his way and the things happening round him.

'O my dear son! Lo! though it be but the weight of a grain of mustard-seed, and though it be in a rock, or in the heavens, or in the earth, Allah will bring it forth. Lo! Allah is subtle. Aware. O my dear son! Establish worship and enjoin kindness and forbid inequity, and persevere, whatever may befall thee. Lo! that is of the steadfast heart of things. Turn not thy cheek in scorn toward folk, nor walk with pertness in the land. Lo! Allah loves not braggarts and boasters.' Sura XXXI (Luqman), verses 16-18

The Role of Muslim Women
Article Seventeen

The Muslim women have a no lesser role than that of men in the war of liberation; they manufacture men and play a great role in guiding and educating the [new] generation. The enemies have understood that role, therefore they realize that if they can guide and educate [the Muslim women] in a way that would distance them from Islam, they would have won that war. Therefore, you can see them making consistent efforts [in that direction] by way of publicity and movies, curricula of education and culture, using as their intermediaries their craftsmen who are part of the various Zionist Organizations which take on all sorts of names and shapes such as: the Freemasons, Rotary Clubs, gangs of spies and the like. All of them are nests of saboteurs and sabotage. Those Zionist organizations control vast material resources, which enable them to fulfill their mission amidst societies, with a view of implementing Zionist goals and sowing the concepts that can be of use to the enemy. Those organizations operate [in a situation] where Islam is absent from the arena and alienated from its people. Thus, the Muslims must fulfill their duty in confronting the schemes of those saboteurs. When Islam will retake possession of [the means to] guide the life [of the Muslims], it will wipe out those organizations which are the enemy of humanity and Islam.

Article Eighteen

The women in the house and the family of Jihad fighters, whether they are mothers or sisters, carry out the most important duty of caring for the home and raising the children upon the moral concepts and values which derive from Islam; and of educating their sons to observe the religious injunctions in preparation for the duty of Jihad awaiting them. Therefore, we must pay attention to the schools and curricula upon which

Muslim girls are educated, so as to make them righteous mothers, who are conscious of their duties in the war of liberation. They must be fully capable of being aware and of grasping the ways to manage their households. Economy and avoiding waste in household expenditures are prerequisites to our ability to pursue our cause in the difficult circumstances surrounding us. Therefore let them remember at all times that money saved is equivalent to blood, which must be made to run in the veins in order to ensure the continuity of life of our young and old.

'Lo, men who surrender unto Allah, and women who surrender and men who believe and women who believe, and men who obey and women who obey, and men who speak the truth and women who speak the truth and men who persevere (in righteousness) and women who persevere and men who are humble and women who are humble, and men who give alms and women who give alms, and men who fast and women who fast, and men who guard their modesty and women who guard [their modesty], and men who remember Allah much and women who remember Allah has prepared for them forgiveness and a vast reward.' Sura 33 (Al-Ahzab, the Clans), verse 35

The Role of Islamic Art in the War of Liberation
Article Nineteen

Art has rules and criteria by which one can know whether it is Islamic or Jahiliyya art. The problems of Islamic liberation underlie the need for Islamic art which could lift the spirit, and instead of making one party triumph over the other, would lift up all parties in harmony and balance.

Man is a strange and miraculous being, made out of a handful of clay and a breath of soul; Islamic art is to address man on this basis, while Jahili art addresses the body and makes the element of clay paramount. So, books, articles, publications, religious exhortations, epistles, songs, poems, hymns, plays, and the like, if they possess the characteristics of Islamic art, have the requisites of ideological mobilization, of a continuous nurturing in the pursuance of the journey, and of relaxing the soul. The road is long and the suffering is great and the spirits are weary; it is Islamic art which renews the activity, revives the movement and arouses lofty concepts and sound planning. The soul cannot thrive, unless it knows how to contrive, unless it can transit from one situation to another. All this is a serious matter, no jesting. For the umma fighting its Jihad knows no jesting.

Social Solidarity
Article Twenty

Islamic society is one of solidarity. The Messenger of Allah, be Allah's prayer and peace upon him, said:

'What a wonderful tribe were the Ash'aris! When they were overtaxed, either in their location or during their journeys, they would collect all their possessions, and then would divide them equally among themselves.'

This is the Islamic spirit which ought to prevail in any Muslim society. A society which confronts a vicious, Nazi-like enemy, who does not differentiate between man and woman, elder and young ought to be the first to adorn itself with this Islamic spirit. Our enemy pursues the style of collective punishment of usurping people's countries and properties, of pursuing them into their exiles and places of assembly. It has resorted to breaking bones, opening fire on women and children and the old, with or without reason, and to setting up detention camps where thousands upon thousands are interned in inhuman conditions. In addition, it destroys houses, renders children orphans and issuesoppressive judgements against thousands of young people who spend the best years of their youth in the darkness of prisons. The Nazism of the Jews does not skip women and children, it scares everyone. They make war against people's livelihood, plunder their moneys and threaten their honor. In their horrible actions they mistreat people like the most horrendous war criminals. Exiling people from their country is another way of killing them. As we face this misconduct, we have no escape from establishing social solidarity among the people, from confronting the enemy as one solid body, so that if one organ is hurt the rest of the body will respond with alertness and fervor.

Article Twenty-One

Social solidarity consists of extending help to all the needy, both materially and morally, or assisting in the execution of certain actions. It is incumbent upon the members of the Hamas to look after the interests of the masses the way they would look after their own interests. They must spare no effort in the implementation and maintenance of those interests, and they must avoid playing with anything that might effect the future generations or cause damage to their society. For the masses are of them and for them, their strength is [ultimately] theirs and their future is theirs. The members of Hamas must share with the people its joys and sorrows, and adopt the demands of the people and anything likely to fulfill its interests and theirs. When this spirit reigns, congeniality will deepen, cooperation and compassion will prevail, unity will firm up, and the ranks will be strengthened in the confrontation with the enemy.

The Powers which Support the Enemy
Article Twenty-Two

The enemies have been scheming for a long time, and they have consolidated their schemes, in order to achieve what they have achieved. They took advantage of key elements in unfolding events, and accumulated a huge and influential material wealth which they put to the service of implementing their dream. This wealth [permitted them to] take over control of the world media such as news agencies, the press, publication houses, broadcasting and the like. [They also used this] wealth to stir revolutions in various parts of the globe in order to fulfill their interests and pick the fruits. They stood behind the French and the Communist Revolutions and behind most of the revolutions we hear about here and there. They also used the money to establish clandestine organizations which are spreading around the world, in order to destroy societies and carry out Zionist interests. Such organizations are: the Freemasons, Rotary Clubs, Lions Clubs, B'nai B'rith and the like. All of them are destructive spying organizations. They also used the money to take over control of the Imperialist states and made them colonize many countries in order to exploit the wealth of those countries and spread their corruption therein.

As regards local and world wars, it has come to pass and no one objects, that they stood behind World War I, so as to wipe out the Islamic Caliphate. They collected material gains and took control of many sources of wealth. They obtained the Baffour Declaration and established the League of Nations in order to rule the world by means of that organization. They also stood behind World War II, where they collected immense benefits from trading with war materials and prepared for the establishment of their state. They inspired the establishment of the United Nations and the Security Council to replace the League of Nations, in order to rule the world by their intermediary. There was no war that broke out anywhere without their fingerprints on it:

'...As often as they light a fire for war, Allah extinguishes it. Their efforts are for corruption in the land and Allah loves not corrupters.' Sura V (Al-Ma'ida - the Tablespread), verse 64

The forces of Imperialism in both the Capitalist West and the Communist East support the enemy with all their might, in material and human terms, taking turns between themselves. When Islam appears, all the forces of Unbelief unite to confront it, because the Community of Unbelief is one.

'Oh ye who believe! Take not for intimates others than your own folk, who would spare no pain to ruin you. Hatred is revealed by [the utterance of] their mouth, but that which their breasts hide is greater. We have made plain for you the revelations if you will understand.' Sura III, (Al-Imran), verse 118

It is not in vain that the verse ends with God's saying: 'if you will understand.'

PART IV

Our Position Vis-a-Vis the Islamic Movements
Article Twenty-Three

The Hamas views the other Islamic movements with respect and appreciation. Even when it differs from them in one aspect or another or on one concept or another, it agrees with them in other aspects and concepts. It reads those movements as included in the framework of striving [for the sake of Allah], as long as they hold sound intentions and abide by their devotion to Allah, and as along as their conduct remains within the perimeter of the Islamic circle. All the fighters of Jihad have their reward.

The Hamas regards those movements as its stock holders and asks Allah for guidance and integrity of conduct for all. It shall not fail to continue to raise the banner of unity and to exert efforts in order to implement it, [based] upon the [Holy] Book and the [Prophet's] Tradition.

'And hold fast, all of you together, to the cable of Allah, do not separate. And remember Allah's favor unto you how ye were enemies and He made friendship between your hearts so that ye became as brothers by His grace; and (how) ye were upon the brink of an abyss of fire, and He did save you from it. Thus Allah makes clear His revelations unto you, that happily ye may be guided.' Sura III (Al-'Imran), verse 102

Article Twenty-Four

Hamas will not permit the slandering and defamation of individuals and groups, for the Believers are not slanderers and cursers. However, despite the need to differentiate between that and the positions and modes of conduct adopted by individuals and groups whenever the Hamas detects faulty positions and modes of conduct, it has the right to point to the mistake, to denigrate it, to act for spelling out the truth and for adopting it realistically in the context of a given problem. Wisdom is roaming around, and the Believer ought to grasp it wherever he can find it.

'Allah loves not the utterance of harsh speech save by one who has been wronged. Allah is ever Hearer, Knower. If you do good openly or keep it secret, or give evil, lo! Allah is forgiving, powerful.' Sura IV (Women), verses 147-148

The National (wataniyya) Movements in the Palestinian Arena
Article Twenty-Five

[Hamas] reciprocated its respect to them, appreciates their condition and the factors surrounding them and influencing them, and supports them firmly as long as they do not owe their loyalty to the Communist East or to the Crusader West. We reiterate to every one who is part of them or sympathizes with them that the Hamas is a movement of Jihad, or morality and consciousness in its concept of life. It moves forward with the others, abhors opportunism, and only wishes well to individuals and groups. It does not aspire to material gains, or to personal fame, nor does it solicit remuneration from the people. It sets out relying on its own material resources, and what is available to it, [as it is said] 'afford them the power you can avail yourself of.' [All that] in order to carry out its duty, to gain Allah's favor; it has no ambition other than that.

All the nationalist streams, operating in the Palestinian arena for the sake of the liberation of Palestine, may rest assured that they will definitely and resolutely get support and assistance, in speech and in action, at the present and in the future, [because Hamas aspires] to unite, not to divide; to safeguard, not to squander; to bring together, not to fragment. It values every kind word, every devoted effort and every commendable endeavor. It closes the door before marginal quarrels, it does not heed rumors and biased statements, and it is aware of the right of self-defense.

Anything that runs counter or contradicts this orientation is trumped up by the enemies or by those who run in their orbit in order to create confusion, to divide our ranks or to divert to marginal things.

'O ye who believe! If an evil-liver bring you tidings, verify it, lest ye smite some folk in ignorance and afterward repent of what ye did.' Sura XLIX (Al Hujurat, the Private Apartments), verse 6

Article Twenty-Six
The Hamas, while it views positively the Palestinian National Movements which do not owe their loyalty to the East or to the West, does not refrain from debating unfolding events regarding the Palestinian problem, on the local and international scenes. These debates are realistic and expose the extent to which [these developments] go along with, or contradict, national interests as viewed from the Islamic vantage point.

The Palestine Liberation Organization
Article Twenty-Seven
The PLO is among the closest to the Hamas, for it constitutes a father, a brother, a relative, a friend. Can a Muslim turn away from his father, his brother, his relative or his friend? Our homeland is one, our calamity is one, our destiny is one and our enemy is common to both of us. Under the influence of the circumstances which surrounded the founding of the PLO, and

the ideological invasion which has swept the Arab world since the rout of the Crusades, and which has been reinforced by Orientalism and the Christian Mission, the PLO has adopted the idea of a Secular State, and so we think of it. Secular thought is diametrically opposed to religious thought. Thought is the basis for positions, for modes of conduct and for resolutions. Therefore, in spite of our appreciation for the PLO and its possible transformation in the future, and despite the fact that we do not denigrate its role in the Arab-Israeli conflict, we cannot substitute it for the Islamic nature of Palestine by adopting secular thought. For the Islamic nature of Palestine is part of our religion, and anyone who neglects his religion is bound to lose.

'And who forsakes the religion of Abraham, save him who befools himself?' Sura II (Al-Baqra - the Co), verse 130

When the PLO adopts Islam as the guideline for life, then we shall become its soldiers, the fuel of its fire which will burn the enemies. And until that happens, and we pray to Allah that it will happen soon, the position of the Hamas towards the PLO is one of a son towards his father, a brother towards his brother, and a relative towards his relative who suffers the others pain when a thorn hits him, who supports the other in the confrontation with the enemies and who wishes him divine guidance and integrity of conduct.

Your brother, your brother! Whoever has no brother, is like a fighter who runs to the battle without weapons. A cousin for man is like the best wing, and no falcon can take off without wings.

Article Twenty-Eight

The Zionist invasion is a mischievous one. It does not hesitate to take any road, or to pursue all despicable and repulsive means to fulfill its desires. It relies to a great extent, for its meddling and spying activities, on the clandestine organizations which it has established, such as the Freemasons, Rotary Clubs, Lions, and other spying associations. All those secret organizations, some which are overt, act for the interests of Zionism and under its directions, strive to demolish societies, to destroy values, to wreck answerableness, to tofter virtues and to wipe out Islam. It stands behind the diffusion of drugs and toxics of all kinds in order to facilitate its control and expansion.

The Arab states surrounding Israel are required to open their borders to the Jihad fighters, the sons of the Arab and Islamic peoples, to enable them to play their role and to join their efforts to those of their brothers among the Muslim Brothers in Palestine.

The other Arab and Islamic states are required, at the very least, to facilitate the movement of the Jihad fighters from and to them. We cannot fail to remind every Muslim that when the Jews occupied Holy Jerusalem in 1967 and stood at the doorstep of the Blessed Aqsa Mosque, they shouted with joy:

'Muhammad is dead, he left daughters behind.'

Israel, by virtue of its being Jewish and of having a Jewish population, defies Islam and the Muslims.

'Let the eyes of the cowards not fall asleep.'

National and Religious Associations, Institutions, the Intelligentsia, and the Arab and Islamic Worlds
Article Twenty-Nine
Hamas hopes that those Associations will stand by it on all levels, will support it, adopt its positions, boost its activities and moves and encourage support for it, so as to render the Islamic peoples its backers and helpers, and its strategic depth in all human and material domains as well as in information, in time and space. Among other things, they hold solidarity meetings, issue explanatory publications, supportive articles and tendentious leaflets to make the masses aware of the Palestinian

issue, the problems it faces and of the plans to resolve them; and to mobilize the Islamic peoples ideologically, educationally and culturally in order to fulfill their role in the crucial war of liberation, as they had played their role in the defeat of the Crusades and in the rout of the Tartars and had saved human civilization. How all that is dear to Allah!

'Allah has decreed: Lo! I verily shall conquer, I and my messengers. Lo! Allah is strong, Almighty.' Sura LVIII (Al-Mujadilah), verse 21

Article Thirty
Men of letters, members of the intelligentsia, media people, preachers, teachers and educators and all different sectors in the Arab and Islamic world, are all called upon to play their role and to carry out their duty in view of the wickedness of the Zionist invasion, of its penetration into many countries, and its control over material means and the media, with all the ramifications thereof in most countries of the world.

Jihad means not only carrying arms and denigrating the enemies. Uttering positive words, writing good articles and useful books, and lending support and assistance, all that too is Jihad in the path of Allah, as long as intentions are sincere to make Allah's banner supreme.

'Those who prepare for a raid in the path of Allah are considered as if they participated themselves in the raid. Those who successfully rear a raider in their home, are considered as if they participated themselves in the raid.' (Told by Bukhari, Muslim, Abu Dawud and Tirmidhi.)

The Members of Other Religions, The Hamas is a Humane Movement
Article Thirty-One
Hamas is a humane movement, which cares for human rights and is committed to the tolerance inherent in Islam as regards

137

attitudes towards other religions. It is only hostile to those who are hostile towards it, or stand in its way in order to disturb its moves or to frustrate its efforts.

Under the shadow of Islam it is possible for the members of the three religions: Islam, Christianity and Judaism to coexist in safety and security. Safety and security can only prevail under the shadow of Islam, and recent and ancient history is the best witness to that effect. The members of other religions must desist from struggling against Islam over sovereignty in this region. For if they were to gain the upper hand, fighting, torture and uprooting would follow; they would be fed up with each other, to say nothing of members of other religions. The past and the present are full of evidence to that effect.

'They will not fight you in body safe in fortified villages or from behind wells. Their adversity among themselves is very great. Ye think of them as a whole whereas their hearts are diverse. That is because they are a folk who have no sense.' Sura 59 (Al-Hashr, the Exile), verse 14

Islam accords his rights to everyone who has rights and averts aggression against the rights of others. The Nazi Zionist practices against our people will not last the lifetime of their invasion, for 'states built upon oppression last only one hour, states based upon justice will last until the hour of Resurrection.'

'Allah forbids you not those who warred not against you on account of religion and drove you not out from your houses, that you should show them kindness and deal justly with them. Lo! Allah loves the just dealers.' Sura 60 (Al-Mumtahana), verse 8.

The Attempts to Isolate the Palestinian People
Article Thirty-Two

World Zionism and Imperialist forces have been attempting, with smart moves and considered planning, to push the Arab countries, one after another, out of the circle of conflict with

Zionism, in order, ultimately, to isolate the Palestinian People. Egypt has already been cast out of the conflict, to a very great extent through the treacherous Camp David Accords, and she has been trying to drag other countries into similar agreements in order to push them out of the circle of conflict.

Hamas is calling upon the Arab and Islamic peoples to act seriously and tirelessly in order to frustrate that dreadful scheme and to make the masses aware of the danger of coping out of the circle of struggle with Zionism. Today it is Palestine and tomorrow it may be another country or other countries. For Zionist scheming has no end, and after Palestine they will covet expansion from the Nile to the Euphrates. Only when they have completed digesting the area on which they will have laid their hand, they will look forward to more expansion, etc. Their scheme has been laid out in the Protocols of the Elders of Zion, and their present [conduct] is the best proof of what is said there.

Leaving the circle of conflict with Israel is a major act of treason and it will bring curse on its perpetrators.

'Who so on that day turns his back to them, unless maneuvering for baffle or intent to join a company, he truly has incurred wrath from Allah, and his habitation will be hell, a hapless journey's end.' Sura 8 (Al-Anfal - Spoils of War), verse 16

We have no escape from pooling together all the forces and energies to face this despicable Nazi-Tatar invasion. Otherwise we shall witness the loss of [our] countries, the uprooting of their inhabitants, the spreading of corruption on earth and the destruction of all religious values. Let everyone realize that he is accountable to Allah.

'Whoever does a speck of good will bear [the consequences] and whoever does a speck of evil will see [the consequences].'

Within the circle of the conflict with world Zionism, the Hamas regards itself the spearhead and the avant-garde. It joins its efforts to all those who are active on the Palestinian scene, but more steps need to be taken by the Arab and Islamic peoples and Islamic associations throughout the Arab and Islamic world in order to make possible the next round with the Jews, the merchants of war.

'We have cast among them enmity and hatred till the day of Resurrection. As often as they light a fire for war, Allah extinguishes it. Their effort is for corruption in the land, and Allah loves not corrupters.' Sura V (Al-Maidah - the Table spread), verse 64

Article Thirty-Three

The Hamas sets out from these general concepts which are consistent and in accordance with the rules of the universe, and gushes forth in the river of Fate in its confrontation and Jihad waging against the enemies, in defense of the Muslim human being, of Islamic Civilization and of the Islamic Holy Places, primarily the Blessed Aqsa Mosque. This, for the purpose of calling upon the Arab and Islamic peoples as well as their governments, popular and official associations, to fear Allah in their attitude towards and dealings with Hamas, and to be, in accordance with Allah's will, its supporters and partisans who extend assistance to it and provide it with reinforcement after reinforcement, until the Decree of Allah is fulfilled, the ranks are over-swollen, Jihad fighters join other Jihad fighters, and all this accumulation sets out from everywhere in the Islamic world, obeying the call of duty, and intoning 'Come on, join Jihad!' This call will tear apart the clouds in the skies and it will continue to ring until liberation is completed, the invaders are vanquished and Allah's victory sets in.

'Verily Allah helps one who helps Him. Lo! Allah is strong, Almighty.' Sura XXII (Pilgrimage), verse 40

PART V - THE TESTIMONY OF HISTORY

Confronting Aggressors Throughout History
Article Thirty-Four

Palestine is the navel of earth, the convergence of continents, the object of greed for the greedy, since the dawn of history. The Prophet, may Allah's prayer and peace be upon him, points out to that fact in his noble hadith in which he implored his venerable Companion, Ma'adh ibn Jabi, saying:

'O Maadh, Allah is going to grant you victory over Syria after me, from Al-Arish to the Euphrates, while its men, women, and female slaves will be dwelling there until the Day of Resurrection. Those of you who chose [to dwell] in one of the plains of Syria or Palestine will be in a state of Jihad to the Day of Resurrection.'

The greedy have coveted Palestine more than once and they raided it with armies in order to fulfill their covetousness. Multitudes of Crusades descended on it, carrying their faith with them and waving their Cross. They were able to defeat the Muslims for a long time, and the Muslims were not able to redeem it until their sought the protection of their religious banner; then, they unified their forces, sang the praise of their God and set out for Jihad under the Command of Saladin aiAyyubi, for the duration of nearly two decades, and then the obvious conquest took place when the Crusaders were defeated and Palestine was liberated.

'Say (O Muhammad) unto those who disbelieve: ye shall be overcome and gathered unto Hell, an evil resting place.' Sura III (Al-Imran), verse 12

This is the only way to liberation, there is no doubt in the testimony of history. That is one of the rules of the universe and one of the laws of existence. Only iron can blunt iron, only the true faith of Islam can vanquish their false and falsified faith. Faith can only be fought by faith. Ultimately, victory is reserved to the truth, and truth is victorious.

'And verily Our word went forth of old unto Our Bordmen sent [to warn]. That they verily would be helped. And that Our host, they verily would be the victors.' Sura 38 (Al-Saffat), verses 171-3

Article Thirty-Five

Hamas takes a serious look at the defeat of the Crusades at the hand of Saladin the Ayyubid and the rescue of Palestine from their domination; at the defeat of the Tatars at Ein Jalut where their spine was broken by Qutuz and Al-Dhahir Baibars, and the Arab world was rescued from the sweep of the Tatars which ruined all aspects of human civilization. Hamas has learned from these lessons and examples, that the current Zionist invasion had been preceded by a Crusader invasion from the West; and another one, the Tatars, from the East. And exactly as the Muslims had faced those invasions and planned their removal and defeat, they are able to face the Zionist invasion and defeat it. This will not be difficult for Allah if our intentions are pure and our determination is sincere; if the Muslims draw useful lessons from the experiences of the past, and extricate themselves for the vestiges of the [Western] ideological onslaught; and if they follow the traditions of Islam.

EPILOGUE

The Hamas are Soldiers
Article Thirty-Six

The Hamas, while breaking its path, reiterates time and again to all members of our people and the Arab and Islamic peoples, that it does not seek fame for itself nor material gains, or social status. Nor is it directed against any one member of our people in order to compete with him or replace him. There is nothing of that at all. It will never set out against any Muslims or against the non-Muslims who make peace with it, here or anywhere else. It will only be of help to all associations and organizations which act against the Zionist enemy and those who revolve in its orbit.

Hamas posits Islam as a way of life, it is its faith and its yardstick for judging. Whoever posits Islam as a way of life, anywhere, and regardless of whether it is an organization, a state, or any other group, Hamas are its soldiers, nothing else.

We implore Allah to guide us, to guide through us and to decide between us and our folk with truth.

'Our Lord! Decide with truth between us and our folk, for Thou are the best of those who make decisions.' Sura VII (Al-Nraf - the Heights), verse 89

Our last call is: Thanks to Allah, the Lord of the Universe.
(From Rafael Yisraeli, in Y. Alexander and H. Foxman, eds, *The 1988-1989 Annual on Terrorism* (The Netherlands: Kluwer Academic Publishers.)

POSTSCRIPT

The terrorists responsible for the World Trade Center in 1993 were under the orders of Ramzi Yousef of the Jihad Organization. Their mission was deemed a failure as, in the words of Yousef, 'they did not topple the buildings.'

What may have just appeared to be wishful thinking on the part of Yousef, turned into a devastating reality several years after his arrest in Pakistan. On September 11, 2001, the famous towers were brought crashing down to earth in the aftermath of the most brutal terrorist attack in history. Few will be able to forget the scenes broadcast around the world of the two hijacked airliners as they slammed into the sides of the towers, killing thousands of innocent Americans as they went about their business in New York. The same organization also sent another airliner crashing into the side of the Pentagon in Washington on the same day. The fundamentalists had finally completed the mission they began in 1993.

The body of evidence points to links between the attacks of 1993 and 2001. When Yousef's computer was seized in the Philippines, references were found concerning the disappointment over the bombers' inability to completely destroy the twin towers. The disgrace of their failure in their sworn duty to Allah was not only theirs, but also their families'. While in the Philippines, Yousef was developing tactics to attack commercial airliners with a view to blowing them up.

The two brothers who carried out the 1993 bombing stated, while in custody, that their goal was to kill over 100,000 Americans when their target building toppled over to the other building. There can be little doubt that the World Wide Fundamentalist Movement has had the most visible monument to America's economic might as its main target for many years. The destruction of the World Trade Center was to be the means of punishing America for its perceived evil, arrogance and domination of the world market.

However, the 2001 attack will be the rebirth and amalgamation, I believe, of America's and the world's attack on terrorist violence.

ADDITIONAL SOURCES

The *New York Times*

The *New York Post*

The *New York Daily News*

The *Newark Star Ledger*

The *Jersey Journal*

The *Congressional Record*

US Military Intelligence

The US Secret Service

The US Customs Service

The Federal Bureau of Investigation

Interpol

The Central Intelligence Agency

The Port Authority of NY/NJ

The Heritage Age Foundation: The Changing Face of Middle Eastern Terrorism, by James Phillips

Additional Sources

Annual editions *Violence and Terrorism of 1999 and 2000*, Dushkin, McGraw-Hill

Two Seconds Under The World: Terror Comes To America: by Jim Dwyer, et al

Blair Fensterstock Esq & Partners, Lead Counsel Plaintiffs Committee, New York, New York

The Truth about Hamas, Ahmad Rashad

The parking lot at the World Trade Center.

The parking lot at the World Trade Center.

Bombing site at the World Trade Center.

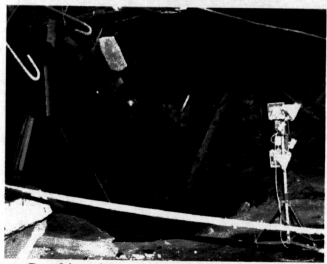

Bombing site at the World Trade Center.

Holy Warriors in central Afghanistan.

Holy Warriors in Afghanistan, cleaning weapons.

Holy Warrior guarding camp.

Afghanistan Holy Warriors having breakfast.